P9-DUM-364

809.933
B730

REFLECTIONS OF THE HOLOCAUST IN ART AND LITERATURE

Edited by
Randolph L. Braham

WITHDRAW

Social Science Monographs, Boulder
and
The Csengeri Institute for Holocaust Studies
of the Graduate School and University Center of
The City University of New York
Distributed by Columbia University Press, New York

1990

LIBRARY ST. MARY'S COLLEGE
182616

Holocaust Studies Series

Randolph L. Braham, Editor
The Institute for Holocaust Studies
The Graduate School and University Center
The City University of New York

Previously published books in the Series:
  Perspectives on the Holocaust, 1982
  Contemporary Views on the Holocaust, 1983
  Genocide and Retribution, 1983
  The Hungarian Jewish Catastrophe: A Selected and Annotated Bibliography, 1984
  Jewish Leadership During the Nazi Era: Patterns of Behavior in the Free World, 1985
  The Holocaust in Hungary—Forty Years Later, 1985
  The Origins of the Holocaust Christian Anti-Semitism, 1986
  The Halutz Resistance in Hungary, 1942–1944, 1986
  The Tragedy of Hungarian Jewry: Essays, Documents, Depositions, 1986
  The Treatment of the Holocaust in Textbooks, 1987
  The Psychological Perspectives of the Holocaust and of Its Aftermath, 1988

The Holocaust Studies Series is published in cooperation with the Institute for Holocaust Studies. These books are outgrowths of lectures, conferences, and research projects sponsored by the Institute. It is the purpose of the Series to subject the events and circumstances of the Holocaust to scrutiny by a variety of academics who bring different scholarly disciplines to the study.

The first three books in the Series were published by Kluwer-Nijhoff Publishing of Boston.

Copyright © 1990 by Randolph L. Braham
ISBN 0-88033-965-9
Library of Congress Catalog Card Number 89-62260
Printed in the United States of America

Contents

Introduction v

Etty Hillesum: A Story of Spiritual Growth
Irving Halperin 1

The Holocaust Poetry of Aaron Zeitlin in Yiddish and Hebrew
Emanuel S. Goldsmith 17

Samuel Beckett's Wandering Jew
Rosette C. Lamont 35

German-Jewish Writers on the Eve of the Holocaust
Diane S. Spielmann 55

Women Writers and the Holocaust: Strategies for Survival
Ellen S. Fine 79

Ashes and Hope: The Holocaust in Second Generation American Literature
Alan L. Berger 97

Fictional Facts and Factual Fictions: History in Holocaust Literature
Lawrence L. Langer 117

Holocaust and Autobiography: Wiesel, Friedländer, Pisar
Joseph Sungolowsky....................................... 131

Art of the Holocaust: A Summary
Sybil Milton 147

Jewish Art and Artists in the Shadow of the Holocaust
Luba K. Gurdus... 153

Contributors.. 165

Introduction

Perhaps no other historical event has elicited such a voluminous scholarly, artistic, and literary response as has the Holocaust. The short time span since the end of World War II makes this all the more remarkable.

The bulk of the artistic and literary outpouring of the first postwar decades was martyrological-lacrymological in nature. Countless sketches and paintings, as well as a plethora of historical and literary accounts, reflected the survivors' recollections and perceptions of their ordeal during the many phases of the Holocaust. Collectively, they also reflected the survivors' commitment to bear witness, to inform the world—and succeeding generations—about the horrors of the Nazi era. In pursuit of this goal many chose the media of art, poetry, and fiction; others relied on more objective avenues of expression, including the historical-personal narrative.

With the coming of age of the children of the survivors, the Holocaust-related artistic-literary creativity acquired a new dimension. The writers and artists of what has come to be called the Second Generation, joined by a considerable number of their non-Jewish colleagues the world over, found inspiration not only in the multifaceted yet unique story of the Holocaust, but also in the postwar behavior and attitudes of the survivors. Belletristic accounts of the Holocaust became intertwined with subtle psychological portrayals of the survivors. Authors began to weave into their literary accounts aspects of the trauma many survivors could not easily shake. They exploited for their literary endeavors many of the psychological-pathological symptoms that psychiatrists have identified as part of the "survivor syndrome." A considerable number of novels and fictionalized historical accounts that appeared during the past decade reflect elements of this syndrome: the failure or inability of survivors to talk about their experiences with their children or grandchildren, their severe and persevering guilt complexes, their depressive moods and morose behavior, and their anxiety and anhedonia.

A few representative samples of this genre are analyzed in three of the essays included in this volume, the twelfth in the Holocaust Studies Series of the Emeric and Ilana Csengeri Institute for Holocaust Studies.

The first part of the volume is devoted to critical-literary analyses of individual writers and poets. The first of the three essays in this section deals with Etty Hillesum, a chronicler and martyr of the Holocaust in The Netherlands. Relying on her diaries and letters that were published in two volumes in the mid-1980s, Professor Irving Halperin traces Ms. Hillesum's spiritual development from her first Amsterdam diary entries in 1941 to her last Westerbork entries written shortly before her deportation to Auschwitz in 1943. The second essay, written by Professor Emanuel S. Goldsmith, is devoted to an analysis of the Yiddish and Hebrew Holocaust-related poetry of Aaron Zeitlin, one of the leading authors of the twentieth century writing in these languages. In her evaluation of *Waiting for Godot*, the final piece in this section, Professor Rosette C. Lamont provides a fascinating argument in support of her conclusion that Samuel Beckett is in fact "one of the great Holocaust writers of our time."

The second part contains five overview articles. Dr. Diane S. Spielmann provides a literary overview of some major German-Jewish writers of the immediate pre-Holocaust era, focusing on Hugo Bettauer, Lion Feuchtwanger, Arthur Landsberger, and Arthur Schnitzler. Professor Ellen S. Fine devotes her piece to an evaluation of women writers, and of the traumas and survival strategies used by women in concentration camps. With respect to the latter, she focuses on spiritual resistance, including the use of literature. Professor Alan L. Berger attempts to decode the Holocaust literature of the Second Generation, convinced that such decoding will help "reveal much about the literary, psychosocial, and theological dimensions of post-Auschwitz Judaism in America." His subjects of analysis include such well-known Second Generation writers as Carol Ascher, Barbara Finkelstein, Thomas Friedmann, Julie Salamon, and Art Spiegelman. In calling his essay "fictional facts and factual fictions," Professor Lawrence L. Langer aims to demonstrate the existence of "a symbiotic kinship between actual and imaginative truth in the literature of the Holocaust." He demonstrates persuasively that a major task of Holocaust criticism is "to clarify the complex bond, in the minds of both author and audience, linking the oppressions of history to the impressions of art." Professor Joseph Sungolowsky provides an incisive evaluation of the autobiographical accounts of three world-renowned survivors of the Holocaust: Saul Friedländer, Samuel Pisar, and Elie Wiesel.

The last part includes two articles dealing with reflections of the Holocaust in art. In a succinct yet informative overview, Dr. Sybil Milton identifies Holocaust-related art as a central element for an understanding of the Nazi era. Whether produced in death or labor camps, in prisons or in hiding, the drawings, sketches, and paintings of the artist-victims constitute—by the very nature of their visual power—a unique treasure and a formidable source for the under- standing of the Holocaust. Dr. Luba K. Gurdus reviews the predicament of Jewish artists during the Holocaust, focusing on those trapped in the ghettos and death camps of Poland. She provides not only a perceptive description of the various art schools that flourished—for a while at least—in spite of the unspeakable conditions, but also of some of the artistic creations of that tragic era. The chilling images of Jewish martyrdom in these paintings and drawings will remain etched in the minds of viewers.

The publication of this volume would not have been possible without the support of many people. I would like to express my gratitude first of all to the contributors. Through the expertise reflected in their essays, they individually and collectively advanced the cause of Holocaust studies. I would also like to express my indebtedness to President Harold M. Proshansky and Dean Solomon Goldstein of the Graduate School and University Center of The City University of New York for their encouragement and support. I would like to acknowledge the generosity of the many contributors to the Special Holocaust Fund, including Valerie and Frank Furth, Eva and Norman Gati, Doris and Louis Glick, and Marcel Sand. I am grateful to all of them for their continuing interest in, and support for, Holocaust studies. Finally, I would like to express my thanks to Emeric and Ilana Csengeri for their generosity and friendship.

Randolph L. Braham
July 1989

Etty Hillesum:
A Story of Spiritual Growth

Irving Halperin

The jasmine behind my house has been completely ruined by the rains and storms of the last few days, its white blossoms are floating about in muddy black pools on the low garage roof. But somewhere inside me the jasmine continues to blossom undisturbed, just as profusely and delicately as ever it did. And it spreads its scent round the House in which You dwell, oh God. You can see, I look after You, I bring You not only tears and my forebodings on this stormy, grey Sunday morning, I even bring you scented jasmine. And I shall bring You all the flowers I shall meet on my way and truly there are many of these. (*Diaries* 152)

This prayer to God was written by Etty Hillesum in the summer of 1942. The writer of extraordinary diaries and letters, she has been described as the adult counterpart of Anne Frank. Like Anne, Etty believed in the existence of a just and loving God, the meaningfulness and beauty of human life, the benificence of Nature, the importance of keeping a diary. Like Anne, she loved Holland and the Dutch people. And like her younger counterpart, she achieved an unusually large measure of spiritual growth in a brief span of time and despite the pressures of dehumanizing circumstances.

Born in 1914, Etty was 28 years old when she died in Auschwitz. She came from a highly educated and cultivated family of assimilated Dutch Jews: her father was a classical scholar and the headmaster of a *gymnasium*; one brother was a brilliant pianist, another brother a gifted practitioner of medicine. After receiving a law degree from the University of Amsterdam, she enrolled in its Faculty of Slavonic Languages as a graduate student of Russian language and literature. A passionate reader, she was especially devoted to the works of Rilke ("my poet," she would speak of him), Dostoyevsky, Tolstoy, St.

Augustine, Jung. Just before the war, she left her parents' home in Deventer and moved into a South Amsterdam household. In March 1941, nine months after the Germans had occupied Holland, at a time when Dutch Jews were ordered to wear the yellow star, she began keeping a diary. Etty spent much of 1943, the last year of her life, in Westerbork, a transit camp in northeastern Holland and the last stop before Auschwitz for over 100,000 Dutch Jews. From there, she continued to write letters to friends beyond the barbed wire.

Shortly before her death, she turned over the diaries (with instructions to find a publisher for them if she did not survive) to a friend; he eventually interested a publisher, and the diaries were published in Holland in 1981, creating an instant literary event. An English translation under the title, *An Interrupted Life: The Diaries of Etty Hillesum 1941–1943*, appeared in 1984.[1] An English translation of her collected letters appeared under the title, *Letters from Westerbork*, in 1986.[2]

Etty Hillesum's diaries and letters are today being read by an international audience. What sets them apart from many eyewitness accounts and personal narratives written by those who survived the Holocaust and by others who did not is that a highly intelligent, sensitive, and talented writer intensely ponders issues concerned with religion, morality, faith, love, community. Her writings are a stunning achievement of the human spirit in the darkest days of the twentieth century.

My purpose here is to examine Etty's spiritual development from the first diary entries in 1941 when she is frequently depressed, confused, and not a little self-absorbed to both the last entries of 1943 and the letters from Westerbork when she appears steadily calmer, clearer, unshaken in her belief that life is meaningful, and increasingly attentive to the tragic plight of the doomed Jewish community.

*   *   *

As the first diary entries of March 1941 reveal, Etty is becoming emotionally involved with a charismatic psychologist in his fifties, Julius Spier, a refugee from Nazi Germany who had trained under Carl Jung and who had a reputation for reading hands and palms with insight. She had sought professional help from him for what she called her "spiritual constipation." Part of her therapy consisted of wild wrestling matches with Julius, a practice employed in that era by some West European psychotherapists. However one may question certain aspects of his professional work, the fact is that he did encourage Etty to keep writing, and he guided her efforts to cope with frequent spells of depression, headaches, stomach ailments and nausea (some of these symptoms were, as eventually she herself would recognize, psychosomatic in origin). She possessed enough self-aware-ness to recognize that she had an "unholy father-complex" about older men and that Julius, as guru and man, was flawed ("My dear spoilt man" she refers to him in the diaries). While acknowledging her dependence on Spier, she resents the compulsion to find her identity through him; she would like to be free of the need to seek Absolute Love from a man. Not without much conflict on both their parts (he tries to stay faithful to his fiancée in London, and she fears sex will undermine their teacher–disciple relationship), they became lovers. Still, determined not to remain a passive partner, Etty comes to draw on her own strength, and they eventually relate to each other as equals.

As late as the spring of 1942, at a time of increasing restrictions on the populace by the Occupation, Etty, by her own admission, finds life fairly pleasant. "I don't think there's another person in all Holland who has it as easy, at least that's how it seems to me" (122). She confesses to feeling guilty about the masses who must stand in long queues for food, while she is economically free (she earns some money by tutoring students, and her expenditures for food, rent and entertainment are modest) to enjoy bicycling, concerts, reading and writing at leisure, strolling along the city's canals, and observing the visual beauty of Amsterdam, especially its world of flowers, which she describes with a sensuous verbal imagination reminiscent of Colette's artistry: "I should like to write about yellow marsh-marigolds, my chestnut twigs, that have stopped blooming now, their small hands stretched out as gracefully as a dancer's and at at the same time raised so defensively towards the sky" (101).

In the early entries there is ample expression of Etty's belief in a universal love. She declares that one should not hate the Germans, not only because man is made in the image of God, but also because "hatred of Germans poisons everyone's mind" (8). Hearing someone curse, "let the bastards drown, the lot of them," she impulsively throws her arms around that person, as though to stifle this outburst of hatred (8). If there is but one decent German somewhere, she argues, it is unjust to malign an entire people; rather than hate the Germans for their brutality, one ought to hate only the evil that is within one's self. As late as September 1942, in a letter to a friend, she professed to have "much love . . . for Germans and Dutchmen, Jews and non-Jews, for the whole of mankind—there is more than enough to go around" (*Letters*, 9).

Etty expressed these sentiments some two years before she and her family were transported to a death camp and well before she realized that the Nazis were bent on not just enslaving but in fact systematically destroying European Jewry.

Meanwhile, apart from her involvement with Spier and her scholastic activities, she focuses on the act of reading. When she can lose herself in the works of her favorite writers, she feels calm and centered. Are not their writings as real, a higher reality, she speculates, than the present realities of the Occupation? For her a poem by Rilke is "as real and important as a young man falling out an aeroplane" (34). So it is that we see her reading at her desk, which she calls "the most beautiful place on earth." On it, beside a vase full of ox-eye daisies, faded tea roses, a geranium and pine cones, are books by some of her favorite writers: Rilke, Dostoyevsky, Tolstoy, Pushkin, St. Augustine, Jung. Their writings strike Etty as a confirmation of her view that life is meaningful and beautiful.

She realizes that her intense attraction to the insights of certain writers stems from her uncertainties and confusions. She searches their writings for some "great redeeming formula" to bring order and clarity to her inner turmoil. At the same time, she grasps what an antidote might be for this dependency: "what does it matter whether I study one page more or less of a book? If only I listened to my own rhythm and tried to live in accordance with it" (61). Moreover, she senses that something in her unconscious is protesting at such woolly abstractions in her lexicon as "purpose," "mankind," "solution of problems." "I find them pretentious," she writes, and adds with a touch of disarming self-deprecation: "But then I'm such an ingenuous and dull young woman still so lacking in courage" (29). In this context, she is quick to acknowledge that her views about the beauty of life may be so much sophomoric theorizing. In short, she knew that she had not yet been tested. All too soon, she would be.

Torn by self-doubt, troubled by her complicated relationship with Spier, Etty increasingly turns to prayer while kneeling on the floor of her room. In one improvised prayer, which is representative of the tone of her religious fervor, she pledges to accept whatever struggles and difficulties are before her:

> God, take me by Your hand, I shall follow you dutifully, and not resist too much. I shall evade none of the tempests life has in store for me, I shall try to face it all as best I can. But now and then grant me a short respite. . . . I don't want to be anything special, I only want to try to be true to that in me which seeks to fulfill its promise. . . . And if I cannot be, because it is not in my nature, then I must face

that as well. In any case I must not try to fool myself. And I must keep within my own limitations. And remember that I alone can set these. (52–53)

If she is a long way from attaining clarity and inner peace, her spiritual development nevertheless moves slowly forward through a process of organic growth—the gradual, unhurried, cumulative unfolding that her beloved Rilke advocated in his *Letters to a Young Poet* as necessary for living a creative life. She finds herself complaining much less often about being unhappy and confused. What has been disparate and fragmented within, she has faith, will eventually come together.

The diary entries of early 1942 also reveal Etty's closer attention to the darkening circumstances of the Jewish community. More and more "No Jews" signs are posted in shops. Jews are prohibited from sitting in cafes, traveling by tram, walking in the open country, being in the streets past the curfew hour of eight, using swimming pools, hockey fields, tennis courts. On observing how eight people occupy one small room in the Jewish district, she is honest enough to question whether she could still cling to her belief that life is beautiful if she were forced to live in similar conditions.

Days of oppression, humiliation, extreme danger—and yet on certain evenings it seems hard to believe that it is wartime when she looks out through the open window of her bedroom and inhales the jasmine-scented air and feels "as if life with all its mysteries was close to me, as if I could touch it. I had the feeling that I was resting naked against the breast of life, and could feel her gentle and regular heartbeat. I felt safe and protected" (115). Of one such evening she writes: "The sky within me is as wide as the one stretching above my head. I believe in God and I believe in man and I say so without embarrassment" (122).

*   *   *

The wheels of Hitler's genocidal machine are turning swiftly. Rumors are widespread: British radio reports that 700,000 Jews may have perished in Germany and in the occupied countries. Reflecting on this report, Etty predicts—and this, tragically, would come to pass for many Holocaust survivors—that "even if we stay alive we shall carry the wounds with us throughout our lives" (127). Then she adds, in what obviously is intended as a symbolic statement, "I have already died a thousand deaths in a thousand concentration camps. I know about everything and am no longer appalled by the latest reports.

In one way or another I know it all. And yet I find life beautiful and meaningful. From minute to minute" (127).

Well, she could not possibly know "everything"; not about Westerbork, not about Auschwitz. Even with her gift of prescience, she could not have pictured the kinds of trials that were before her. And Etty herself must have realized that such statements were not based on experiential reality. After writing that "Suffering has always been with us, does it really matter what form it comes? All that matters is how we bear it and how we fit it into our lives," in the next breath she challenges the validity of her own declaration: "Am I merely an armchair theorist safely ensconced behind my desk, with my familiar books around me and the jasmine outside? Is it all theory, never tested in practice?" (129).

Whether her notion here about the meaning of suffering is merely "theory" or not, what does ring clear is that now she no longer has any illusions about the fate of Dutch Jewry. "They are out to destroy us completely, we must accept that and go on from there," she writes. "Today I am filled with terrible despair, and I shall have to come to terms with that as well. Even if we are consigned to hell, let us go there as gracefully as we can. I did not really want to put it so blandly" (130).

Largely because of what is happening in the streets, the widening Nazi plague, something inside her, she feels, has crystallized: she resolves to look beyond her desk at the disquieting facts of daily life in the Occupation. Describing this stage of her inner development, Etty avers: "I have come to terms with life. . . . By 'coming to terms with life' I mean: the reality of death has become a definite part of my life; my life has, so to speak, been extended by death, by my looking death in the eye and accepting it, by accepting destruction as part of life and no longer wasting my energies on fear of death or the refusal to acknowledge its inevitability" (131–132). In expressing these sentiments about death, Etty had not yet seen a dead person. In her own words, she has a "virginal" sense of death. "Just imagine: a world sown with a million corpses, and in twenty-seven years I have never seen a single one" (132). In Westerbork, she would not be spared the sight of corpses.

*   *   *

More and more Dutch Jews are being called up for "labor camps" in, presumably, Germany. Etty expects to receive her call-up papers soon. She is certain, given her medical history of susceptibility to anemia, colds, fatigue, and stomach ailments, that in a camp she would break down within three days. And if she should die there?

In two of the most resonant sentences in the diaries, she states: "It doesn't matter whether my untrained body will be able to carry on, that is really of secondary importance; the main thing is that even as we die a terrible death we are able to feel right up to the very last moment that life has meaning and beauty, that we have realized our potential and lived a good life. I can't really put it into words" (138).

Now she begins making practical and what she calls "inner preparations" for a call-up. What would she do on receiving papers with orders to leave in, say, a week's time? First, she would try to see her parents and reassure them. Then she would have a dentist fill her cavities ("For that really would be awful; suffering from a toothache out there") (148). She would have her hair cut short, discard her lipstick and have a pair of trousers and a jacket made from leftover winter coat material. How would she pack all her underwear, blankets and food into the one allowable suitcase for the three days' journey to a camp? And what about her books? Certainly she would have to find room for the Bible, the "rugged and tender, simple and wise" Bible which gave her much pleasure and instruction and which could help her through difficult days, as it had for a writer with whom she identified, Dostoyevsky, when he was incarcerated in a Siberian prison. Yes, and there would have to be room in the suitcase for Rilke's *Letters to a Young Poet*, two small dictionaries, Tolstoy's folk tales, Dostoyevsky's *The Idiot*.

That is what she would do by way of practical preparations. But what about others who would be called up with her—how to help them? Would she be able to reassure the parents whose children would be going without them to "unknown destinations"? (Why speak of unknown destinations? Etty writes, "Wherever I go, won't there be the same earth under my roving feet and the same sky with now the moon and now the sun, not to mention all the stars, above my grateful head?") (178) by promising, "Don't worry, I'll look after your children"? (145). Directly after posing this question, she pulls herself up sharply, "But I am still talking in much too philosophical, much too bookish a way, as if I had thought it all up to make life more pleasant for myself" (146).

Etty's inner preparations for call-up include a vow to bear witness, to become a chronicler of what is happening in Holland and elsewhere. Here her tone is, uncharacteristically, almost militant: "And I shall wield this slender fountain pen as if it were a hammer and my words will have to be so many hammer-strokes with which to beat out the story of our fate and of a piece of history as it is and never was before" (146). And if in a camp she is not able to write? Then she

would carry her observations within. In any event, she counsels
herself, there is no cause for despair; even from behind barbed wire
one would be able to exercise inner freedom ("there will always be
a small patch of sky above, and there will always be enough space
to fold two hands in prayer" (153).

At this point, July 1942, Etty's friends urge her to go into hiding
instead of waiting to be called up. (On one occasion, according to
Jan G. Gaarlandt, who wrote the introduction to *Letters from Westerbork*,
she resisted an attempt by friends to take her by force to a safe
address.) When she refuses to do so, they accuse her of passivity and
unworldly naïveté. To this charge her response is that she does not
want to be "saved" when so many thousands have to go to labor
camps. ". . . it is sheer arrogance to think oneself too good to share
the fate of the masses" (150). Besides, she is certain that the enemy
cannot harm her as long as she feels safe in God's arms. "They may
well succeed in breaking me physically, but no more than that. I may
face cruelty and deprivation the likes of which I cannot imagine in
even my wildest fantasies. Yet all this is as nothing to the immeasurable
expanse of my faith in God and my inner receptiveness" (149). To
those who would call her an incorrigible dreamer or mystic, she would
reply that though her realities might be different from what many
people would call reality, still they *are* realities.

                              *   *   *

We come now to a phase of Etty's life which would push her away
from, as she wrote, "her peaceful desk into the midst of the cares
and sufferings of this age" (159). Prodded by a close friend, she
reluctantly applies to the Jewish Council office in Amsterdam (reluctantly because she realizes that the Wehrmacht-controlled Council
has been coerced into transporting Jews to Westerbork) and given a
typist's job. In undertaking this assignment, she hopes to keep her
family and friends off the transport lists. Working there is unpleasant:
a hundred people are crowded into a small, noisy room; her typing
chores are monotonous; her fellow workers are preoccupied with
intrigues and petty grievances. There are times when she doesn't
think she can endure another day in this atmosphere. But then she
would tell herself that she has no right to complain when she is well
off compared with some of her friends who are forced to work in
factories for 60 hours a week. So she resolves to hold on there.

Reviewing her inner progress over a year's time, Etty affirms that
she possesses a new calmness, and this enables her to endure the
dispiriting work at the Jewish Council. "Had all of this happened to
me only a year ago, I should certainly have collapsed within three

days, committed suicide or pretended to a false kind of cheerfulness" (160).

In the late summer of 1942, Etty volunteered to accompany the first group of Dutch Jews to Westerbork transit camp, which was located on a heath in northeastern Netherlands near the German border. Her status as an employee of the Jewish Council permitted her to come and leave there at will. Within a half square kilometer of huts and wooden barracks, dust, mud and human misery, fields of regal purple lupines grew beside the barbed wire of this camp. Westerbork had been built in 1939 to accommodate no more than 1500 displaced German Jews, but after 1942 it bulged with as many as 10,000 inmates at any one time. From July 1942 to September 1944, 93 transports, on the average of a thousand men, women, children and invalids in each one, left the camp for "unknown destinations." A transport consisted of sealed freight cars with some 70 people to a car. The "passengers" slept, when they could sleep, on hard floors. Paper mattresses were provided for invalids. A single bucket for bodily needs was placed in the middle of a car. The journey usually took three days.

At her writing desk in Amsterdam, Etty had felt safe and peaceful. In Westerbork, before going there, she wondered whether she would continue to believe that life is beautiful and meaningful? And would she have the will and stamina to describe what she observed there? She would not find answers to these questions during her brief initial encounter with Westerbork, although later, back in Amsterdam, Etty would speak of this experience as having been "the two richest and most intense months" of her life (174). There would be further "rich" (if this is an apt word for describing life in Westerbork!) and "intense" months on her subsequent returns to the camps, and through these experiences her ability as a writer would be exercised and validated.

At the end of August 1942, she arrived in Amsterdam in time to be at the side of her dying lover. Julius Spier's health had been steadily deteriorating. His death affected Etty profoundly. Not that she had deluded herself into supposing that they had a future together; he had a fiancée in London, and there was the great difference in their ages. More important, even before his illness, she had recognized that the ultimate importance of Julius in her life was not that of a lover or therapist but rather that of a "mediator" between herself and God. It was from him that she had first learned "to speak the name of God without embarrassment" (169).

Kneeling beside Julius's death bed, she admonishes herself to be grateful both for the great happiness she had known in their relationship and also for his having been spared the additional suffering that the

Occupation most certainly would have inflicted upon him. She addresses his spirit in these words: "You could be impatient about small things, but about the important things you were so patient, so infinitely patient. . . . All the bad and the good that can be found in a man were in you—all the demons, all the passions, all the goodness, all the love" (171).

Looking at the first dead person that she has ever seen, Etty vows to "live on with that part of the dead that lives forever, and I shall rekindle into life that of the living which is now dead, until there is nothing but life, one great life, oh God" (172).

*   *   *

In the aftermath of Julius Spier's death and during her recuperation from an illness that she had contracted at Westerbork, Etty would look back at her brief stay in the transit camp with, astonishingly, almost a feeling of homesickness, as witness the September 23, 1942 diary entry which contains this memorable passage: "At night the barracks sometimes lay in the moonlight, made out of silver and eternity: like a plaything that had slipped from God's preoccupied hand" (180). This stunning trope clearly attests to her rich sensibility. Here it is as though she has dreamed that Westerbork is merely a temporary aberration within God's universe. This recollection also suggests that Etty sensed it was morally imperative for her to be back in Westerbork, sharing the fate of her people.

In November 1942, bearing a special permit from the Jewish Council, she returned to the transit camp in the role of a social worker. Much of her activity consisted of looking after patients in the hospital barracks. Although her permit from the Council allowed her to journey to Amsterdam to pick up medical supplies and to deliver messages from the camp's inmates, in Westerbork she did not receive preferential privileges. Like the other inmates, she slept on the same plank beds in barracks insufferably hot and stifling in summer and bitterly cold in winter and ate the same miserable scraps of food. At night she lay awake on a triple-deck bed amid women and girls who were dreaming aloud, tossing and turning, sobbing. Perhaps there were times when she would look around at such nightmarish scenes and wonder whether they were the handiwork of a feverish imagination. She had traveled a considerable distance from her peaceful desk in Amsterdam to the plank beds of Westerbork.

Before coming to the transit camp, she had vowed to be a chronicler, "the eyes and ears of a piece of Jewish history." Now, in Westerbork, among Jews from all over the Netherlands, she wants to be "the thinking heart of the barracks" (*Letters*, xv). But how to describe the

indescribable? To depict the miserable and grotesque conditions here—
so grotesque that they border on the unreal—she writes to a friend,
one would have to be able to write fairy tales (*Letters*, 88).

She has come a long way from a privileged life in Amsterdam,
and yet Etty is sometimes severely critical of her attitude in Westerbork.
Astonishingly, for such a serious and responsible person, she speaks
of herself as frivolous and easy-going and too much the mere spectator
of the misery in the camp, as though she were an outsider on a brief
visit. "I have fallen short in all ways, my real work has not even
begun," she berates herself (183).

But the fact is that her "real work" had begun: she was a scrupulous
chronicler of the Westerbork hell. In her diaries and letters, powerfully
and painstakingly recorded, are some of the most horrifying and tragic
sights and scenes in the literature of the Holocaust. In a letter dated
August 24, 1943, we read of mothers sitting helplessly beside the
cots of their sick children; "the piercing screams of babies dragged
from their cots in the middle of the night" (208); the distress of
abandoned children who are ignored by women who have enough
worries looking after their own families; a partly paralyzed young
girl who has just learned that she has been selected for a transport
("We look at each other for a long moment. It is as if her face has
disappeared, she is all eyes. Then she says in a level, grey little voice,
'Such a pity isn't it? That everything you have learned in life goes
for nothing. . . . How hard it is to die'" (209); a deranged looking
woman who cries out to Etty: "That isn't right, how can that be
right, I've got to go and I won't even be able to get my washing dry
by tomorrow. And my child is sick, he's feverish, can't you fix things
so that I don't have to go? . . . Can't you hide my child for me? Go
on, please, won't you hide him, he's got a high fever, how can I
possibly take him along?" (210–211); a young mother selected for
transport warns her screaming baby, "If you don't behave yourself,
mummy won't take you along with her!" (210); a colleague of Etty's
squatting beside the bed of her dying mother, who has swallowed
poison (211).

Scenes from an inferno, and in its midst an elderly woman asks
Etty, "Could you tell me, please, could you tell me, why we Jews
have to suffer so much?" Etty cannot bring herself to reply, but later
she cries out, silently, "God Almighty, what are You doing to us?"
(*Letters*, 129). And there were the times when the screaming of sick
and terrified children would especially get to her, and she would
despair, seeing "nothing but blackness and nothing makes any sense
at all" (*Letters*, 58).

In Westerbork Etty wasn't merely an observer and chronicler; she wanted to help others, to be, in her words, "a balm on many wounds." So we see her going from barracks to barracks, squeezing tomato juice for babies, calming distraught mothers, doling out coffee among hundreds of inmates, comforting a hundred-year-old woman by listening to her life story. Such selfless acts probably account for why some survivors of Westerbork still speak with awe of her "shining personality" (*Letters*, xv).

How did Etty view the camp's persecutors? In a departure from the times in Amsterdam when, in an all-embracing profession of love for humanity, she would admonish her friends not to hate the Occupation's oppressors because they too were made in the image of God, she is revulsed and frightened by the faces of a squad of guards who go about their grisly business on the night before a transport. "Oafish, jeering faces in which one seeks in vain for even the slightest trace of human warmth," she writes. "At what fronts did they learn their business? In what punishment camps were they trained?" (215). She simply cannot reconcile her notion of humanity in the image of God with those brutal faces.

The intensity of her life in Westerbork takes its toll. Etty becomes anemic, has to lie on her bunk for hours at a time, and finally is brought to an Amsterdam hospital for the treatment of gallstones. "You have too cerebral a life, it's bad for your health, your constitution isn't up to it," a Dutch doctor scolds her (184). While admitting to her "demonic" intensity, Etty feels that the doctor doesn't grasp that she calms herself by reading. She is especially moved by St. Augustine, viewing him as "full of simple devotion in his love letters to God" (193).

Etty was to administer more "balm on wounds" with the arrival of her parents and brother Mischa in Westerbork on June 21, 1943. Given their genteel background, she fears that they will not survive the camp's hardships. But they soon cope admirably. For example: her father gives lessons in Greek and Latin and reads Homer and Ovid to two young patients in the hospital barracks. All the while, Etty futilely considers ways by which her family might be kept off the transport lists, but, realistically, she knows that the trains leave the camp every week and that the quotas must be filled. In the meantime, she does whatever she can to lighten their burdens. With misgivings, because she hesitates to impose upon her Amsterdam friends who are not finding it easy to get by in a wartime economy of strict rationing, Etty makes what she calls mundane requests. "I feel awful, but there's no help for it," she writes in a letter. "What we need urgently for Father is rusks and things like that. He hasn't eaten for days and must be helped back to his usual form slowly; the camp bread is terrible (*Letters*, 108–109). In another letter to this same friend, after apologizing for "causing a lot of trouble," she asks, "Could you get some little Antifones at a chemist's? They're the things you put in your ears to block out noise. In Mother's barracks it is very noisy at night, with a lot of small children who are sick—really there's nowhere here that isn't noisy—and now she wants to try sleeping with the earplugs" (*Letters*, 114).

For her family everything, for herself very little. And when she does ask something for herself the tone of the request is that of a self-denying person. "Do you know what I would still love to have here?" she writes to a friend. The "what" are a woolen dressing gown, a felt hat and a knitted dress, all of which are stored in her former residence. "It's fairly cold here sometimes," she explains, "and in case I should suddenly be put on a transport—you never know what will happen." Here Etty breaks off the request, as though regretting having made it. She was never to receive these garments. Five days after this letter was posted, Etty was placed on a transport to Auschwitz.

As late as four months before her death, she continues to maintain that life is good. Making light of her "little bit of physical discomfort" behind barbed wire, she writes that Westerbork cannot deprive her of her freedom. From a bunk she would look up at the sky over the camp to see some gulls in flight and think, "They are like free thoughts in an open mind" (*Letters*, 106). She intuits that she will not survive, but no matter. What is important is to reflect on *how* one meets death. "What tens and tens of thousands before us have borne, we can also bear. For us, I think, it is no longer a question of living, but of how one is equipped for one's extinction" (*Letters*, 100).

Then it was the turn of the Hillesums. On September 7, 1943, Etty, her parents and Mischa—her older brother was brought to Westerbork later, and he too did not survive—were placed on a crowded transport to "somewhere" in Poland. Long before, she had steeled herself for this moment ("Even if we are consigned to hell, let us go there as gracefully as we can.")

And that is how she went, according to Jopie Vleeschouwer, a friend of hers and also an inmate of Westerbork, wrote of Etty's departure in a letter: "Talking gaily, smiling, a kind word for everyone she met on the way, full of sparkling humor, perhaps just a touch of sadness, but every inch the Etty you knew so well. 'I have my diaries, my little Bible, my Russian grammar and Tolstoy with me and God knows what else'. . . . I only wish I could describe for you exactly how it happened and with what grace she and her family left!" (221).

From a window in a wagon goods train, Etty threw a postcard which was recovered later; it read:

> Opening the Bible at random I find this: "The Lord is my high tower." I am sitting on my rucksack in the middle of a full freight car. Father, Mother, and Mischa are a few cars away. In the end, the departure came without warning. On sudden special orders from The Hague. We left the camp singing . . . . (*Letters*, 146).

She died in Auschwitz on November 30, 1943.

In what state of mind she perished we cannot know, though one can imagine that she went with her kind of grace. What we do know is that the trajectory of her spiritual journey was from that of a self-absorbed, private person to one who willingly and heroically assumed large communal responsibilities. The diaries and letters written in Westerbork indicate that Etty no longer was romantically theorizing on the meaning of suffering or thirsting after spiritual adventures; rather she seemed to have attained a genuine inner peace. In the camp she made meaningful connections with other Jews and linked herself with their destiny. Her writing was both a defense against despair, the death of the spirit, and a form of spiritual resistance against the oppressors. Through her writing and her humanity, she praised the sanctity of life. Looking outward, beyond the self, looking squarely and clearly at the historic moment, she had come of age in an age of genocide.

In Amsterdam, at her desk, Etty asserted that life is full of beauty and meaning. In Westerbork, behind barbed wire, she apparently found confirmation for this belief.

> Surrounded by my writers and poets and the flowers on my desk I loved life. And there among the barracks, full of hunted and persecuted people, I found confirmation of my love of life. . . . Not for one moment was I cut off from the life I was said to have left behind. There was simply one great meaningful whole. Will I be able to describe all that one day? (177).

NOTES

1. Etty Hillesum, *An Interrupted Life: The Diaries of Etty Hillesum.* Introduction and notes by Jan G. Gaarlandt. Trans. by Arnold J. Pomerans. New

York: Pantheon Books, 1984. All quotations are referred to parenthetically from this edition and without reference to the title.

2. Etty Hillesum, *Letters from Westerbork*. Introduction and notes by Jan G. Gaarlandt. Trans. by Arnold J. Pomerans. New York: Pantheon Books, 1986. All quotations are referred to parenthetically from this edition and identified by the designation, *Letters*.

The Holocaust Poetry of
Aaron Zeitlin
in Yiddish and Hebrew

Emanuel S. Goldsmith

Some of the most moving documents of the Holocaust are to be found in the poetry and fiction of the victims and survivors. Yiddish and Hebrew letters, in particular, abound in a large body of important works dealing with this tragic event and its aftermath. Aaron Zeitlin (1898–1973), one of the leading Yiddish and Hebrew authors of the twentieth century, made major contributions to this genre in both languages. His large number of Yiddish poems on the Holocaust are contained in the two volumes *Lider fun Khurbn un Lider fun Gloybn* (*Poems of the Holocaust and Poems of Faith*),[1] and the smaller number of Hebrew poems in the volume *Ruah Mimetsulah* (*A Spirit From The Deep*).[2] In addition, Zeitlin produced a long dramatic poem on the Holocaust in Hebrew entitled *Beyn Ha-esh Vehayesha* (*Between Fire and Salvation*),[3] which may be regarded both as his major poetic statement on the Holocaust and as one of the most important works on the subject to appear in any language and in any literary form.

For a survivor like Zeitlin—who lost wife, child, father, brother, and other members of his family—the transformation of pain and horror into verse is not accomplished without pangs of shame and guilt. "Be silent and shudder when I scream!" commands the image of a survivor who castigates the poet for trivializing this newest of Israel's devastations. Out of the bitterness and anguish of his soul, the poet responds:

If we, the last Jews,
Are left with naught save words,
How can you have the heart

17

To want to remove our last shirt,
Our little miserable words?

Zeitlin concludes this brief confessional poem by turning to his readers
who probably share the poet's guilt for deriving aesthetic satisfaction
from the reading of poems about the Holocaust.

So again,
Last Jews, Jews of words, my weak brethren,
Again I bring you naught save words,
Naught save poems.

(Lider fun Khurbn. . . , vol. I, p. 59)

In the poem "Israel of Hosts" the poet writes:

To you, folk of flame
And folk of ocean,
I pray
And direct my devotions.
Holy, holy, holy is Israel,
Israel of Hosts!

(Ruah Mimetsulah, p. 374)

It is no accident that the poet applies the appelations and phrases
usually reserved for the Almighty alone to slaughtered Jewry ("Mag-
nified and sanctified be the great name of Israel"). The Holocaust
renders God, even in the company of the celestial hosts, a lonely
God returning home to His heavens at night, after each day of defeat
on the battlefield. God has become a Job, but a Job without a Creator
to dispute and contend with. When a Jew rises in the transport, en
route to the gas chamber, to kindle memorial lights, others add their
voices to his in reciting the *kaddish* in their own memory. But God
also rises in order to recite the *kaddish* for the world.

The Holocaust leaves the world "without God and without a Jew."

The day lit up
Over the square of a courtyard in Warsaw.
A flock of frightened shadows
Quietly made a run for it
Down the old walls.
The tree, the only tree
Burst out in red laughter.
A wind conveyed
Odors from Gentile distances.

For Reb Berish, the old Hasid,
Birds and sun and remote places
Were matters for idolators.
The graybeard knew
That birds and sun and all such things
that play and shine and laugh
Like a thousand joys
Wait humbly for a Jew
To offer them to God and grant them their fulfillment.

Since he was one of the very pious,
He would rise early
To bring fulfillment to every thing:
The one tree in the courtyard,
The wind, the morning cloud that shines
Above the old fence walls.
In his hands,
The hands of a weak mortal,
Was the key to the gate—
The gate of Divine kindness.

Where is his prayer? Where his acts of fulfillment?
Murder, murder, murder.
Outside world, outside time, outside place.
The Jew is no more, his voice is not heard—
And no longer is there anyone
To give meaning to the sun,
To offer the day a God.

(*Lider fun Khurbn. . .* , vol. I, p. 30.)

Even the Angel of Death, who in one of Peretz's dramas conjured the spirits of the dead for the playwright, is unable to do so again. The angel's wings have been destroyed together with the playwright's people. "I am no angel," he says, "but the last groan of a Jew exterminated in Treblinka."

In a survey of the themes of Israeli poetry on the Holocaust, Zevi Dror groups the poems under ten categories: premonition and protest; descriptions of Jewish life before the Holocaust; portrayals of the Holocaust; the call for revenge; castigation of the apathetic world; utilization of symbols and heroes of the Jewish tradition; the turning to God as supreme power; songs of resistance, rebellion and revolt; the Jewish war against the enemy and the aliyah movement; and conclusions drawn from the Holocaust.[4] Zeitlin has written poems in Hebrew and Yiddish which could be classified among all of these categories. But this analysis misses the theme which dominates Zeitlin's Holocaust poetry. That theme is the struggle for faith, the quest for spiritual meaning, and the problem of maintaining belief despite the overwhelming tragedy.

The poetry of the Holocaust may be viewed generally as an attempt to mitigate suffering by giving intense but controlled expression to the tragedy. It represents an effort to preserve sanity by conferring a minimum of order and form on chaos and horror. Zeitlin's poems, however, go beyond this because their overriding concern is the quest for meaning and transcendent faith. Zeitlin affirms the reality of God, the efficacy of prayer, the Messiah, the Millennium, immortality, and the world beyond in his poems. For him there must be a meaning to the gruesome events of our time. In his poetry one hears both the voice of utter and uncompromising despair and the voice of confidence, hope, and faith in God.

The poems of despair are grounded in the awareness of the finality of the Holocaust. Standing on a street in Montreal in midwinter, the poet imagines for a moment that he is in Warsaw again and that his wife is about to turn a corner to meet him. But he knows that she will never ever come again. A sentimental tune that he and his wife were wont to sing in Warsaw hounds him on the streets of New York. "What do you want of me?" he says to the tune. "Everything is over, everything has been gassed. She, too, is no longer mine. She has been betrothed to blazing fire." The poet yearns to hear his wife's voice call his name. How dark and how poor the earth has become since her voice has been silenced! "Send me your voice, call me! and I will carry myself to you as birds carry themselves south in winter." He recalls his wife's tears as he left Poland for the United States, expecting to return in a few months, but in reality never to return. "Everything has vanished. As a nest is dark in wintertime, so my world is empty. Those final tears knew everything. They knew all."

He hears his martyred son in the ghetto relate a dream to his weeping mother:

When father kissed me
For the very last time,
It was early morning
And raining hard.
How far is it, mama, to America?

I had a dream, mama.
Father stands in a yellow hat.
Above him the sun as red as wine.
He opens America for us.
And we enter.

So will it be
If the Germans don't murder us.

Mama, tell me. Why did God
Make Germans?
Don't cry. I just wanted to know.
Do we have a pencil?
I'll draw the sun for you.
I'll draw father
In the yellow hat.
We shall both look
At my dream.

(*Lider fun Khurbn.* . . , vol. I, p. 70f.)

When the war ends, streets are filled with flags and trucks, with shouts of joy and victory. From the gas chambers and crematoria, however, there is only silence. "The war is over and the Jews are over. No, not over. Now begins their silence, the war of the six million."

Zeitlin reaches the lowest depths of personal despair, with the thought that perhaps the game is not worth the candle, that even the end of Messianic redemption fails to justify the means of catastrophic Holocaust. When a pensive angel, with death before his eyes and the cry of millions in his ears, contemplates the final goal of all and proclaims it good, another angel, with tears in his eyes, "who knows of each man's death, and hears the slightest groan," disparages any ultimate redemption. What, asks the poet, if in the world beyond there are Hitlers too? What if there, too, Israel's Prince is devoured by cannibals? What if, even in eternity, blood spurts from a knife?

To the little child and the peaceful animals in the Biblical vision of the End of Days, the poet poses the question: Was it for your sake that God needed Israel's pain and the horror of 2,000 years? Buchenwald and Maidanek? Was it for your sake that the devil had a free hand while Israel was compelled to be burned? Must the poor always be humiliated? Insanity is the answer! "Be destroyed, oh End of Days, as my millions were destroyed!"

The fact that Zeitlin left Poland before the Nazi terrors and was spared the agony of his family and his people weighs upon his conscience as an unbearable source of guilt. "I was not privileged to walk the path of flames together with my people." The sin of remaining alive and the sin of writing poetry are unpardonable. The sense of guilt will poison him until he heeds one of the three figures always at his side who alone can absolve him of his guilt. Too weak to heed the call of suicide, and too insignificant to follow the voice of sanctity, he is even unable to take the path of madness as an escape.

Since life is impossible in such a profane world and death is only a passage to new life, the poet prays that God invent for him an existence between life and death. In the words of Moses he pleads to be erased from God's book. He compares himself to the sun's afterglow at sunset. "I am such an afterglow suspended over the abyss, an afterglow of my nation's sun that set in the sea of blood of Maidanek." Ridden with memories of a world gone up in flames, the poet lives a dual life—as a person in New York and as a shadow in a house in Warsaw which no longer exists. "Souls of the martyred, recite the *kaddish* for me, a corpse who walks about on the earth!"

Zeitlin moves between two poles which may be represented by the references in his poems to Bialik's "In the City of Slaughter" ("The sun shone, the almond tree blossomed, and the slaughterer slew") and the verse from Maimonides with which the martyrs went to their deaths ("I believe with perfect faith in the coming of the Messiah and even though he tarries still do I await his coming daily"). Examples of this are the two poems, written in utter despair during the war years, each of which the poet later modified—in one case with a new stanza and in the other with a new poem.

In the first, written in 1939, God marches forth to destroy the world. The language of vengeance and bloodshed is that of Isaiah 63 ("I trod them in my anger and trampled them in my wrath; their life blood is sprinkled upon my garments and I have stained all my raiment"). But by 1946, when the second part of the poem was written, the poet knows that only "Jacob has been burned to death and Esau has remained." His faith, which formerly bore wings, is battered and bruised. But he cannot abandon his hope for revenge and his belief in divine justice. He dreams that the souls of the dead will be brought down to earth as children, one of whom will be the Messiah.

The second poem, "We Jews Are Not of This World" (1944), takes its title from a statement in which the Hasidic leader, Rabbi Nahman of Bratzlav, sought to explain the world's persecution of Israel. "There may still be Jews below, but Israel is no longer." On this planet Esau alone will praise God with instruments of destruction. The fires of Treblinka have destroyed the prayers of Israel and God, too, is being punished. Yet after the war, with the birth of the State of Israel, the poet experiences a rebirth of faith. He now realizes that the last prayers had not been uttered. "Everything depends on prayer and Jew. There are no last Jews and no final prayers." (*Lider fun Khurbn. . .*, vol. I, p. 53–56).

The essence and strength of Zeitlin's faith derive from the fact that it feeds and grows on the very edges of desperation. The path of faith winds through the lands of despair. Its tears fall on bare foundations of burned-out buildings. But in those very tears a bright dawn is reflected. Faith cannot be found by those who have never known despair.

Zeitlin's poems of complete despair are few. His most powerful evocations of hopelessness are his most convincing demonstrations of faith. In "Post-Maidanek Dream" the poet imagines that he is an atomic scientist standing beside a massive cyclotron. In revenge for the murdered six million, he plots to destroy the earth. An angel, who himself bears a concentration-camp number on his arm, appears to him, soothes him and tells him to recall the names of Jewish children. "A child will heal you," he is told. As the poet brings the names of the martyred children to mind, the figure of a little boy, Koppele, emerges. The angel has commanded the child to be reborn, to build his life anew. The poet warns the child to return whence he came, not to seek a new life in a wicked world which will soon have to be destroyed. The angel proclaims that Koppele must be born again. "Cease from revenge," he calls to the poet. "Leave the earth alone. Restrain the atoms. Koppele must return to hallow God's name for such is God's will." (*Lider fun Khurbn. . .* , 1:89–97).

The poet often confronts his own mood of futility and pessimism:

I defy death with all my might.
Death is nothing but a name.
Are the six million really dead?
They are an ever present flame.

. . .

I am but a thread in the weave.
I began to rot as though dead
When martyrs' voices from Poland said
To me: Live!

. . .

"Jew" and "stop" can't unite, never will.
The meaning of Jew is anti-end.

(*Lider fun Khurbn. . .* , vol. I, p. 150f.)

In the unfathomable pain inflicted on his people, Zeitlin hears the cry that God exists. If tortures such as Israel experienced were impossible, there might not be a God. With such afflictions, however, God's reality is a necessity. Without it, Israel's sufferings would be so hideous and senseless that the earth would reel in drunken madness and disintegrate.

in its land] sharply and clearly, even if it be the only contribution of *Beyn Ha-esh Vehayesha* to Hebrew literature, is enough."[6]

The drama opens with a poem in which the *payyetan*, or Bard, who narrates the plot, reacts to the events, and translates the speech of the protagonists into the language of poetry, links the Holocaust to the destruction of Jerusalem by the Romans 2,000 years ago. This adumbrates one of the major themes of the work—the joining of the Holocaust to the rebuilding of Jerusalem and the rebirth of Israel on its own soil. The work deals with many of the issues we have already confronted in Zeitlin's shorter poems on the Holocaust. Here, however, they take on a new intensity and significance because they are related to Israel's struggle for independence.

In his introduction to the drama, Zeitlin warns the reader not to underestimate those elements which may appear purely literary and contrived. These, he contends, are the very same elements which constitute the essence of the experience he seeks to convey. Zeitlin is referring to the confrontations he stages between the living and the dead of many generations, to his concretization of surrealistic and kabbalistic entities, and to a variety of hermeneutical devices utilized in the poem. The intense suffering and tragedy which the work deals with make the reader open to all attempts at catharsis and render even the most remote efforts at recovery plausible and effective. Of Zeitlin's approach, Isaiah Rabinovich writes that "it is a tradition of Israel that out of the abysses of despair and nothingness man harkens anew to his own existential depths and the voice of God then penetrates from the eclipse in the void. From this point, man must struggle to reconstruct the faith in his heart. . . . Only in the course of this ascending psycho-existential process will he attract the grace which descends from Messianic superconsciousness, from the vision of redemption at the end of days."[7]

On the ruins of the Warsaw Ghetto, Shealtiel, a partisan who has lost his wife and young son in the crematoria, tries to commit suicide but is thwarted in the attempt by the "invisible hands" of past generations. With the aid of *oznayin*, a visionary concretization of the higher functions of eye and ear, Shealtiel witnesses his own trial, during which he discovers that death is an illusion and that justice and retribution do exist in the ultimate scheme of the universe. Awakened to life by this vision, Shealtiel goes to Israel and becomes a commander in the struggle of the *yishuv* against the British. Later he disappears in order to assume the role of a recluse in the synagogue of the medieval mystic Rabbi Isaac Luria in Safed. When the War of Independence erupts, Shealtiel joins those defending Safed from its Arab attackers and helps liberate the city.

Zeitlin fills the poem with numerous other characters, both realistic and imaginary, who embody the problems and hopes of contemporary Jewry in Israel and the Diaspora as well as the longings and dreams of Jews throughout history. Miriam, a fellow survivor, is in love with Shealtiel. She follows him to Palestine with the hope of getting him to leave the country and travel with her around the world. Spurned by Shealtiel, she eventually marries Mister Bloom, a wealthy American Jew who meets her while touring Warsaw with his daughter Laura after the war. Laura is a spoiled young woman, with no roots in her Jewish heritage, who is attracted to Shealtiel and marries him.

In the course of his visionary trial, Shealtiel's murdered wife and child appear to assure him that death is nonexistent and to encourage him to rebuild his life because "everything noble and desirable depends on choosing life" (p. 131). In this vision on the ruins of the Warsaw Ghetto ("the vision on the rock of Israel's mourning"), Shealtiel also sees the martyrs of the Ghetto, the Jewish commander of Masada during the war against the Romans (Eliezer ben Yair), Queen Sabbath, and King David. He witnesses the trial of Doctor Von Tod, the embodiment of the Nazi lust for genocide, at which Satan and the spirits of a dog and a cat testify that

> . . . this brown one
> Did not murder members of his kind alone,
> He destroyed the hope of all of nature's children:
> The forest is bowed and the clod groans,
> The mountain sighs and the grass cries.
> He attempted to restrain the vibrancy
> Of eternally vibrant forces, of mighty powers.

(p. 163)

Numerous other characters appear during scenes depicting Shealtiel's dreams. In the Israeli scenes, the historical figure of Menachem Begin and the Sabra, Shealtiel's fighting companion, make their appearance.

Beyn Ha-esh Vehayesha captivates the reader with the magic of its poetic, dramatic and philosophical dimensions. In terms of aesthetic structure and poetic originality, it is a tour-de-force encompassing a variety of poetic forms and rhyme schemes. Dramatically, it may be viewed as a motion picture script or as a play for a theatre-in-the-round with a revolving stage. Philosophically, it deals cogently with problems such as the meaning of faith, death and immortality after the Holocaust, with the purpose of art, and with the spiritual meaning of Israel reborn. It abounds with reflections on numerous other philosophical and theological issues and contains poetic formulations

LIBRARY ST. MARY'S COLLEGE

of insights into various aspects of Jewish and general life and thought. It unlocks the mind and heart of one of the most sensitive Jewish artists and thinkers of the twentieth century.

Aaron Zeitlin developed a unique world-view born of his own sufferings and those of his people in modern times. The most important contribution of *Beyn Ha-esh Vehayesha* lies in the dramatic and poetic exposition of that *Weltanschauung.* Zeitlin has been described as a philosophical poet with a unique point of view on both Jewish and universal matters which constitutes the basis of a large portion of his poetic work as well as of his articles and essays. But he was primarily a poet. "As a poet he displayed great originality as well as both signs of the influence of world literature and creative and structural elements which he shared with his contemporaries."[8]

Zeitlin saw the essence of Jewish existence in the war against paganism and the longing for redemption.

> To be a Jew means:
> To bring a true redeemer and smash idols.
>
> (p. 186)

These two concerns dominate *Beyn Ha-esh Vehayesha.* Zeitlin sets out to smash the idols of cynicism, doubt, and despair and to replace them with faith in the God of justice, immortality, and deliverance. For Zeitlin the rebirth of Israel in our time contains within it the seeds of the "Dawn of Redemption" (*athalta digeulah*) in which the spirit of martyred Israel will be linked forever to the soul of living Israel. This redemption also contains the beginnings of a new approach to life and art which will bring redemption to all humanity.

> Puny humanity will suddenly
> See the mark of deathlessness, the sign of eternity
> On its forehead, its glorious forehead,
> Withdraw its hand and suddenly become humble.
> It will become ill
> From then on with an illness of longing.
> Longings for transcendence will eat away at it
> Until it is finally exalted.
>
> (p. 220)

As Isaiah Rabinovich writes: "The aesthetic aspect is a very important judicial element in the 'trial' which Shealtiel prepares for himself on the rock in the ghetto. It is clear that this trial in fact involves Zeitlin's self-understanding as a poet, criticism of his own artistic direction before the Holocaust . . . in the empty vacuum of modern art which has also captured the Jewish artist, he holds on to the altar of life which is the Messianic idea."[9]

The principal problems of humanity in the post-holocaust era, an era in which *eyn netsah Yisrael, yesh retsah Yisrael* ("there is no eternity of Israel, only the murdering of Israel"), the problem of God's existence and the problem of Divine goodness are among the issues Shealtiel confronts throughout the poem.

> Without unity and responsibility, can there be immortality
> To life and to deeds? And without immortality
> How will reward be granted and punishment dispensed?
> Without the One God who binds events in a bond
> That is unbreakable, what bridge exists
> Over the howling abyss? Only the absence
> Of all connections is the solution.
>
> (p. 80)

Gradually Shealtiel begins to understand the secret of *lahamam* (an acronym of the words *lo haya mavet me-olam* or "death has never existed"). *Lahamam* is the opposite of the well-known acronym *lahadam* (*lo hayu devarim me-olam*) meaning "these things have never existed." It is also the secret of eternal survival in the Image or Likeness.

> Every situation has its Likeness, both above and below,
> Every reality and every being have their Likeness,
> Your individuality or the individuality of a group or nation,
> Each has its Likeness and the Likeness never ends.
>
> (p. 114)

Shealtiel learns the true meaning of Psalms 30:5, "weeping may tarry for the night, but joy comes with the morning": the weeping that tarries for the night is itself the joy that comes with the morning. He is assured that *"Adonay* has said: I shall restore from smoke, I shall restore from the depths of the sea." Most important, he hears the voice of his dead wife in the ghetto praying the "prayer of perhaps":

> The truth, alas,
> Is clear . . . And yet . . . perhaps . . .
> The Germans will discover
> The bunker
> And no almighty God
> Will come to help . . .

It's clear . . . it's certain . . .
But the beautiful face
Of my lad as he sleeps . . . perhaps . . .
If there be a God,
There must be a continuation
Of my child's life . . . and of mine
For what will he do without me?
I ask only that
In whichever world he exists
Let not my child be separated
From me . . . Let us be together . . . together . . .

                                                              (p. 195)

In the course of his vision, Shealtiel is taught that all wrongs are
set right in Eternity which holds the mysterious key to all existence
and in which reward and punishment are realized. The purpose of
immortality is the repair and improvement of all things; its ultimate
goal is the annihilation of all evil. In Zeitlin's work, the Holocaust,
in its spiritual dimensions, is a conflict between the principles of
nihilism and immortality. His concept of Image or Likeness seeks to
deny the very existence of death as a reality. For Zeitlin, as Hillel
Barzel points out, the mystery of *lahamam* is not an aesthetic abstraction
without concrete meaning. "There is a firm faith here in the eternal
existence of all creatures. Zeitlin actually gives expression to the law
of the preservation of phenomena."[10]

The revenge which Shealtiel seeks will be realized through the
establishment of a country on earth that will be the opposite of the
kingdom of evil-doers.

. . . a country which will not be
Animal-like, devouring all:
It will be a new kingdom inspired by the Divine Presence,
A model-land, the dwelling place of Messiah-men.

                                                              (p. 219)

Shealtiel must marry, bring a child into the world, and struggle for
the establishment of the new country. He must become a partisan of
the Messiah and of the future kingdom. One must struggle for Messiah's
coming by combining prayer and deed in the way God did when He
created the world.

The Creator held His own hand
And let it rest.

He prayed to Himself: "Let there be!"
Then He activated His prayer—and it came to be.

When you battle Amalek—
Combine prayer and deed.
Struggle while you pray
And pray while you struggle.
Without deed, prayer lacks
Power; without prayer
The deed is
Unredeemed.
Unite them—and prevail!

(pp. 212–13)

The poem reaches its dramatic climax in the battle for Safed and its ideological climax in the final dialogue of Shealtiel and "the Sabra." Shealtiel has come to believe that the redemption will be delayed until the establishment in Israel of a new community of seekers of salvation: the community of *shin-mem-lamed-tav*. These four Hebrew letters stand for "two verses which are in truth one": "I keep Maidanek before me always" and "I keep Messiah before me always." (These phrases are Zeitlin's variations on the biblical verse, "I keep the Lord before me always" (Psalms 16:8), which was traditionally engraved or painted above the holy arks in synagogues the world over.) To his Israeli companion's contention that the new state must abandon all Messianic visions, stretch its borders and become stronger than its enemies, Shealtiel responds:

If this land
Becomes just another homeland,
Why shouldn't your son leave it
And go elsewhere on the wide tumultous globe?
If you bequeath to him just another country—what has his soul acquired?
. . .
What need is there for a country that strives not
For a new kind of person,
For a sacred kingdom,
And revolts not against a world that believes in
The lie called death? It will be destroyed,
Nothing of it will remain
If ape-like Jacob
Imitates Esau
And revolts not
Against man-as-he-is

In the name of
Messiah-man, Messiah-people.

(pp. 384–85)

In the course of his vision on the rock in the ghetto, Shealtiel's wife says of their son Elyele:

Yes, in the meantime our little one
Has learned to draw as one draws in Eternity.
His eyes do not see fragments.
He sees every thing about everything,
All ramifications at once,
And his honest eye does not distort
His vision—it is witness and judgement.

(p. 137)

As Isaiah Rabinovich explains, the intuitive-aesthetic perception of little Elyele has in Eternity become a kind of superior knowledge of human and cosmic existence. This knowledge is conveyed through the lips of the child in the Beyond proclaiming that death does not exist; only life exists in Eternity. In the transformation from life to death nothing is lost. "The appearance of each thing, its Likeness, passes into another dimension and in doing so its existence assumes a deeper significance."[11] One might say that in *Beyn ha-esh Vehayesha* Zeitlin's art has itself become "an art of witness, uniting past and present" (p. 378). At the conclusion of the poem, the "Bard" parts from Shealtiel with these words:

In the fire of my pain, my soul brought you forth.
I escorted you from the ruins hence.
I'm sorry we must part. I know
You are but a partial creation
But in you I implanted
My pain, my caring faith,
My life's misfortune—a personal misfortune,
A drop that contains the sea in the sea of
A nation's catastrophe.

(p. 388)

NOTES

1. Aaron Zeitlin, *Lider fun Khurbn un Lider fun Gloybn*. New York: Bergen-Belsen Press, Vol. I., 1967; Vol. II, 1970. All translations from the Yiddish and Hebrew are by the author of this essay.

2. Aaron Zeitlin, *Ruah Mimetsulah*. Tel Aviv: Yavneh, 1975.

3. Aaron Zeitlin, *Beyn Ha-esh Vehayesha*. Tel Aviv: Yavneh, 1970.

4. Zevi Dror, *Nose Hashoah Bashirah Ha-ivrit*. Tel Aviv: Seminar Hakibutsim 1964, p. 14.

5. Joseph Dan, *Hanokhri Vehamandarin*. Ramat-Gan: Massada, 1975, p. 149.

6. *Ibid.*, p. 152.

7. Isaiah Rabinovich, *Behavley Doram*. Tel Aviv: Am Oved, 1959, p. 234.

8. K.A. Bertini, *Sedeh Re-iyah*. Jerusalem: Mosad Bialik, 1977, p. 251F.

9. Rabinovich, *op. cit.*, p. 241.

10. Hillel Barzel, *Shirah Umorashah*. Tel Aviv: Eked, 1971, Vol. I, p. 165.

11. Rabinovich, *op. cit.*, p. 240.

Samuel Beckett's Wandering Jew

Rosette C. Lamont

Much has been said and written about the pilgrimage to Auschwitz, yet nothing ever prepares one for the discovery of the camp's memorial museum—a two-floor red brick building, one of the remaining block houses. Not far from it stands the infamous "hospital," where experiments were carried out on living victims. In yet another building one can visit the underground cell in which Father Kolbe, the priest who was canonized by Pope John Paul II, perished when a camp guard hastened the end of his flickering life with an injection of acid. Father Kolbe, a Polish Catholic priest, had volunteered to take the place of a fellow prisoner, who was condemned with nine others of his block to die slowly of thirst and starvation after an inmate of their block staged an unsuccessful escape. The narrow cell in which the ten hostages were herded is now a shrine.

The most enlightening visit is that of the Auschwitz museum. The ground floor walls are covered with the photographs of those who perished in the camp. One flight up one finds the "display cases," where, behind the large glass cases, is displayed testimony to the carefully orchestrated program of putting to various "practical" uses parts of the human anatomy. Other cases show the personal belongings of the prisoners. For example, one case contains nothing but strands of blond, dark, or gray hair. Tresses and locks fill the large case from top to bottom. Next to this case, a smaller one holds a piece of cloth woven from the women's hair; it is a simple burlap of the kind one might use for sacks, or even a smock or an apron. In another room, a similar large case contains nothing but eyeglasses. Many are broken or twisted. Steel frames are entangled with elegant horn-rimmed ones. The glasses lie in a heap upon a sand base, as though they had just been torn off the faces sent into the gas chambers. Further, one encounters a bizarre display of canes, crutches, artificial limbs. Most are strewn upon the sandy base, while others lean against the back wall, as though their crippled owners had just limped off, out of sight. Perhaps the most Kafkaesque of all these displays is the one which contains only valises and handbags. Again, these are not placed in any kind of order. They have been piled up to look like a junk heap, a piteous remnant of an existence which was once orderly, dignified. Name tags, attached to the handles proclaim their owner. One reads "Kafka."

All of these remnants are metonymies of a mute dirge to those who dame to die in this desolate spot. Yet they are not figures of speech, but terrifying realities, fragments whch speak to us of a relentless dismemberment, a carefully planned and documented annihilation. However, for contemporary readers and theater audiences, there is a striking analogy between the images Beckett creates in his novels and upon the stage and these display cases. They confirmed for me what I had sensed rather than reflected upon for many years: that Samuel Beckett is one of the great Holocaust writers of our time. There are passages in *Waiting for Godot* one can no longer read without realizing how deeply marked they are by this awareness. For example, at the beginning of Act II, Gogo and Didi, who have been debating, or playing at debating, the painfulness of being endowed with thought, state that although they are no longer in "danger of ever thinking any more," they "*have* thought."[1] Having thought once, they are unable to forget. The following passage is a mesmerizing evocation of the post-Second World War, post-Holocaust Europe:

> VLADIMIR: Where are all these corpses from.
> ESTRAGON: These skeletons.
> VLADIMIR: Tell me that.
> ESTRAGON: True.
> VLADIMIR: We must have thought a little.
> ESTRAGON: At the very beginning.
> VLADIMIR: A charnel house! A charnel house!
> ESTRAGON: You don't have to look.
> VLADIMIR: You can't help looking.
> ESTRAGON: True.
> VLADIMIR: Try as one may.
> ESTRAGON: I beg your pardon?
> VLADIMIR: Try as one may.[2]

It has often been said that Beckett is an apolitical writer. As more facts about his life and thought are revealed, however, this judgment appears to be superficial, if not erroneous. We need only recall Beckett's decision to leave the safety of Ireland and return to France at the outbreak of war, and his involvement in the Resistance movement during the German occupation. As to his feelings in regard to Jews, he always had and still has close Jewish friends. In fact, his favorite uncle by marriage was a Jew. In the above passage, it seems obvious that Didi and Gogo are evoking the battlefields of Europe, and most probably the concentration camps. "Charnel house" is repeated twice by Vladimir. Yet Estragon, more of the common man than his philosopher-friend, stresses that people only thought about the horrors of the war and the Holocaust "at the beginning." Human nature is such that it gets used to the unthinkable. Estragon goes so far as to suggest that it would be better to look away. But Vladimir is firm: "You can't help looking." It is human to try to avoid the spectacle of corpses and skeletons, but one does not succeed. Again, it is Vladimir who repeats: "Try as one may."

A couple of years ago, upon my return from Poland, I decided to probe Beckett's reaction to the question of the political in his work. After a moment's hesitation, I made up my mind to tell him about the Auschwitz museum displays. I ventured to say that nothing reminded me more vividly of some of the images he had created upon the stage than these glass cases full of artificial limbs, valises, eye glasses, and empty frames. Even the sandy bottom evoked the desert of *Godot*. The valises in particular reminded me, I said, of Pozzo's luggage, carried by his slave Lucky. Then again, Beckett's heroes in his trilogy (*Molloy Malone Dies, The Unnamable*) are all cripples. They embark upon long voyages even though their legs are failing them, so that they are reduced to crawling. Above all, the character Gogo, in the *Godot* manuscript which I had been able to consult at the Editions Minuit, was called Levi throughout Act I, until Beckett seemed to decide to give him a vaguely universal name.

Beckett did not answer me directly, but he began to talk with deep sorrow about his close friend Alfred Péron who died as a result of having been sent to concentration camp. Péron was arrested when a spy infiltrated the Resistance group in which he and Beckett had worked together. "We were amateurs," Beckett said with his typical smile of self-deprecating irony, "and therefore naïve, vulnerable. We never identified the traitor in our midst. The day Péron was arrested by the Gestapo, his wife managed to send us a telegram of warning. The moment we received it, Suzanne (Beckett's companion, now his wife) and I walked out of our apartment. We took nothing with us. For a day or two we were hidden by friends in Paris while papers were being forged for us. With these we made our way into the 'free zone.'"[3]

In 1942, Samuel Beckett and Suzanne became wanderers. They reached the southern city of Roussillon-de-Vaucluse, where they spent two difficult years. As a foreigner, Beckett could have been denounced and arrested, particularly when Pétain's so-called "free zone" disappeared. Beckett worked on a farm. At night he was writing *Watt*, "in order not to go quite mad,"[4] as he told me. He went on with his Resistance activities, joining a *maquis*. As Alfred Simon writes in his *Beckett*: "The vagabonds Gogo and Didi owe much to the Sam-Suzanne couple without Beckett ever imposing upon us his personal memories of the Occupation of France."[5]

It was at that time, when Beckett led an uprooted, precarious existence, that he must have experienced Freud's apprehension that "*unheimlich* is in some way or other a sub-species of *heimlich*."[6] As a man without a *Heim* (a home), a foreigner in a land which had become, by virtue of enemy occupation, estranged from itself, he must have felt the full significance of "the uncanny." In the South of France, he met others like himself: people torn from their former existence, from their surroundings: people who had become aliens in their own land.

In his essay, "Das Unheimliche," Freud describes and discusses Hoffmann's *Nachstück*, "The Sand Man." There is something strangely prophetic about the unbridled rampage of Coppelius/Coppola, the lawyer who sanctioned the burning of living infants in furnaces, the optician who does not sell glasses but living eyes.

Although the supernatural plays no part in Beckett's *oeuvre*, everyday contemporary reality is tinged with strangeness, and the dead are never out of reach. Often their voices rise, sounding in the mind of lonely, haunted men, such as Beckett's Joe, the guilty creature of his television play, *Dis, Joe*. Our doubles stare at us from mirrors in which we fail to recognize ourselves. Beckett's heroes are driven by forces beyond their control, carried like leaves lifted by the wind, or assigned to a place from which there is no escape, where they wait endlessly.

Although Beckett cannot be called a political writer, history has stamped him with its pain. Yet, Beckett carefully avoids narrowing his scene to a specific time or place. Thus, in *Godot*, the names of the four characters suggest diverse national origins: Vladimir might be Russian, Estragon French, Pozzo Italian, and Lucky British or Irish. Estragon, however, (the name means *terragon* in English), reminds us of the aromatic, bitter herb allied to wormwood. It is appropriate as a replacement for the original name of Levi, particularly since wormwood appears in the Bible in connection with the Apocalypse, and bitter herbs must be tasted by Jews in the course of the ritual Passover meal. The name Estragon ends with "agon," the key scene of conflict in a Greek tragedy. It also significantly echoes "agony." As to the diminutive, Gogo, it is a particularly ironic nickname for one unable to stir from the place where he and his friend Didi are waiting for Godot. If Didi could be the nickname of *Dieu* (the French for God), Gogo might also be that of God. Taken together Gogo and Didi combine to make Godot. Perhaps the two friends are merely waiting for themselves, waiting to be fused into the single human being of which they are the two parts.

If Didi is the thinker of the Gogo/Didi couple, Gogo, the salt of the earth, is also one of the victims of life's absurdity. Beaten at night by unidentified assailants, he comes to accept pain as one of the constant components of existence. Nor can Vladimir protect his friend from being a scapegoat, much as he would like to. Gogo is beaten for no reason. At the beginning of Act II we have the following exchange:

> VLADIMIR: . . . you don't know how to defend yourself. I wouldn't have let them beat you.
> ESTRAGON: You couldn't have stopped them.
> VLADIMIR: Why not?
> ESTRAGON: There were ten of them.
> VLADIMIR: No, I mean before they beat you. I would have stopped you from doing whatever it was you were doing.
> ESTRAGON: I wasn't doing anything.
> VLADIMIR: Then why did they beat you?
> ESTRAGON: I don't know.
> VLADIMIR: Ah no, Gogo, the truth is there are things escape you that don't escape me, you must feel it yourself.
> ESTRAGON: I tell you I wasn't doing anything.
> VLADIMIR: Perhaps you weren't. But it's the way of doing it that counts, the way of doing it, if you want to go on living.
> ESTRAGON: I wasn't doing anything.[7]

Estragon denies any guilt on his part three times, but he also knows that there is "nothing to be done."[8] This declarative statement provides the comical, mock-philosophical opening line of the play. Gogo is commenting on the fact that he is unable to pull off his boots, and the audience watches him struggle through this clown act. But, at the same time, "nothing to be done" could sum up the whole situation of man on this planet. In the above exchange, the comic and the tragic are also interfused, particularly in Vladimir's statement: "it's the way of doing nothing that counts." In fact this comment acquires added significance if one bears in mind Gogo's original name. It suggests that Jews will be persecuted no matter what they do, or fail to do. In the play, it also acquires wider significance. "If you want to go on living," you cannot rely on being guiltless. It is important to be canny, to remain aware of ever–present danger, of the determination of evil people to destroy human life.

Gogo's acceptance of pain makes him a spiritual descendant of Job. In a series of brilliant classes given at Yale University on *The Book of Job,* Elie Wiesel stressed that the book's author shows that Job was an innocent, predestined to suffer. This explains the humility with which he accepts the relentless infliction of physical pain and moral sorrow. Perhaps Beckett also believes that the Jobs of this world revel in their dejection. Vladimir, who has his own afflictions, accuses his friend of being self–centered: "No one suffers but you. I don't count. I'd like to hear what you'd say if you had what I have."[9] Only then does Estragon inquire: "It hurts?"[10] However, when he does, he is no longer a kind of Parsifal, a foolish pilgrim who fails to ask what ails the Fisher King. Nor does he act like Ahasuerus, who, when he was a humble cobbler on the path to Calvary, refused Jesus a moment of rest in his shop.

If the most striking example of physical pain is Job, the symbol of infinite moral suffering might well be the legendary figure of Ahasuerus. Condemned to live forever while moving over the face of the earth till Judgment Day, the wanderer supplanted after the Renaissance the twin figures of Malchus, the High Priest's servant who was sent to seek Jesus for questioning, and that of the officer who dealt Christ a blow in Caiphas' presence. In the Christian tradition, these two men are considered to be mirror images of Judas. However, Ahasuerus was also viewed as a man bent on repentance. A pilgrim, a hermit, the Wandering Jew was also the last living witness to Christ's passion. Unable to share a family meal, to secure shelter, to stop anywhere for a night's rest, he also represents the passage of time, senseless, absurd time, tied to a condition of changelessness. Thus, Gogo and Didi's constant repetition of the phrase "let's go,"[11] as they themselves remain immobile, might be one of the possible interpretations of the myth of the Wandering Jew. For them also nothing changes since there is "nothing to be done."

One of Beckett's striking vaudeville bits of stage business in *Waiting for Godot* is that of Gogo's boots. The first time we see him, sitting on the sand, he is trying to pull them off: They are so tight they might not belong to him. His feet are swelling. At the end of Act I, Gogo leaves his uncomfortable boots downstage, where he will find them on the next day, at the start of Act II. Are they in fact the same ones, or has another pair been substituted while he slept? Act II begins with a comical exchange about this whole problem, the proper identification and attribution of a pair of boots:

VLADIMIR: Where are your boots?
ESTRAGON: I must have thrown them away.
VLADIMIR: When?
ESTRAGON: I don't know.
VLADIMIR: Why?
ESTRAGON (exasperated): I don't know why I don't know!
VLADIMIR: No, I mean why did you throw them away?
ESTRAGON (exasperated): Because they were hurting me!
VLADIMIR: (triumphantly pointing to his boots): There they are! (Estragon looks at the boots). At the very spot where you left them yesterday!
Estragon goes toward the boots, inspects them closely.
ESTRAGON: They're not mine.
VLADIMIR (stupefied): Not yours!
ESTRAGON: Mine were black. These are brown.
VLADIMIR: You're sure yours were black!
ESTRAGON: Well they were a kind of gray.
VLADIMIR: And these are brown. Show.
ESTRAGON (picking up the boots): Well they're a kind of green.[12]

Gray or green, these do not seem to be tight. The boots are probably the same ones. Doubt as to their identity allows for that margin of error which makes them less unbearable. Early in the play, Didi declares: "There's man all over for you, blaming on his boots the faults of his feet."[13]

So much is made of this that we cannot help but wonder: Why boots? Of course it is a sadly funny episode, a vaudeville act not unlike the exchange of the three bowlers. But this emphasis on walking, on being barefoot, suggests the pilgrim's way. At one point, Estragon speaks of "the beauty of the way. And the goodness of the wayfarers."[14] There are echoes here from *Pilgrim's Progress, Everyman,* and the ancient myth of the wanderer. There is also the possibility that Gogo must pull off his boots at that particular spot because he is standing on holy ground. It is he who identifies the lone tree of the set as a bush, insisting on this description:

ESTRAGON: Looks more like a bush.
VLADIMIR: A shrub.
ESTRAGON: A bush.[15]

If it is indeed "a bush," then the bare skeleton of the tree we see in Act I certainly points to the possibility that this bush has been consumed. The fact that it does not look like a burning bush, but a burned bush, may be a feature of Beckett's irony. At the repetition of the word "bush," our minds turn to chapter 3 of *Exodus*, when God tells Moses not to draw nigh, ordering him to put off his shoes since the place where he stands is holy ground. This essentially comic scene, replete with circus gags, also suggests that the two friends, who are living in expectation of Godot's arrival, are already on Godot's land. In fact, Pozzo, whom Estragon has at first taken for Godot, claims that the companions are invading his property:

> POZZO: Waiting? So you were waiting for him?
> VLADIMIR: Well you see—
> POZZO: Here? On my land?[16]

Pozzo belongs to the race of owners, those who believe that the world is their oyster, but even he must admit that "the road is free to all." Here the road is a *via dolorosa*. Could this be the reason why the two companions move only in circles, staying basically on the same spot? Are they not like Malchus who walked around a column, full of deep despair?

As to the name Godot, which has been discussed and puzzled over by so many, it might be derived, as Ruby Cohn pointed out in her early seminal study, from the popular French word for shoes: *godasses, godillots*. When questioned about who Godot might be, Beckett firmly stated: "Had I meant Godot to be God, I would have written God and not Godot."

Although it is highly unlikely that the source for the name Godot can be traced to Balzac's character called Godeau, it is also problematic to assume, as Dr. Hélène Baldwin does in her chapter "The Quest of Vladimir and Estragon" in *Samuel Beckett's Real Silence*, that the title of the play is a direct allusion to Simone Weil's *Waiting for God*. Baldwin goes so far as to state that since Beckett is known as an artist who "relishes the metaphysical, it appears that Godot is God."[17]

Although Beckett is one of the creators of the genre I call "The Metaphysical Farce"—a definition he himself prefers to "Theater of the Absurd"—he is first and foremost a humanist—a man concerned with humanity. His sensitivity to the plight of humanity, his love and loyalty in regard to friends and acquaintances, his interest in politics (not always obvious, but ever present) make of him a kind of exposed nerve. Yet the sense of humor is always there—in his brilliant blue eyes, in the little laugh which fuses from him like a tropism.

Waiting for Godot was written after Beckett finished *Watt*. It took him less than four months, from October 9, 1948, to January 29, 1949. Beckett was working simultaneously on his trilogy: *Molloy*,

Malone Dies, and *The Unnamable.* As he told me in the course of one of our conversations in Paris: "Having completed *Watt* I felt a need to find myself in a space less infinite than that of the novel. By writing a dramatic piece, I stood with my characters in a circumscribed spot, under a certain kind of light. I was in greater control of things." Then he went on to say: "As you will see, when you read my manuscript at the offices of the Editions Minuit, I did not make many changes as I was writing. It is one of these rare works which come spilling out."[18]

Waiting for Godot is marked by the years of exile, secrecy and resistance activity Beckett and Suzanne shared during the German occupation of France. This is how Beckett describes his life after 1939:

> I started writing in French in my mother's room. I had returned home to Ireland to see her after six years of separation. In fact I had at first thought I might teach, but I had no talent for it. So I came home, wagging my tail. There was nothing left to do but be a writer. However, when I heard Chamberlain's speech after Munich I knew it was done for. I wanted to join Suzanne, who wasn't yet my wife, and I did not wish to be cut off from Europe, to stay in Ireland. War had been declared when I got to Dover. There I had quite a time persuading people that I just had to get to France. I pleaded, I implored, and they let me through.
>
> During the Occupation, I was a member of the Resistance. We had a spy in our midst. Most of my comrades were arrested. Alfred Péron was sent to concentration camp. At the time of the Liberation he was still alive. He started on a trek in the direction of France. On the roads survivors resorted to cannibalism. Péron died of exhaustion and starvation. During that time I was in hiding with Suzanne. We worked for a peasant in Vaucluse. I had to pull out the small oak trees which no longer yielded any truffles at their roots. At night, in order not to go mad, I worked on *Watt.*[19]

Physical and moral pain infuse every line of *Godot.* Waiting at that somber time had a special character: one hoped for the end of war, the victory of the Allies, one waited for the end of horror and fear, or simply for the end of waiting. On this level, the play reflects History and Beckett's personal story as well. It is also possible that Beckett recalled the Romantic poet Alphonse de Lamartine's commentary on his poem "L'Immortalité." In 1849, Lamartine wrote: "Toute foi est un calmant, car toute foi est un espérance, et toute espérance rend patient. Vivre, c'est attendre."[20] (Faith has a calming effect for it is a form of hope, and hope lends one patience. To live is to await).

It is in this light that we must view the numerous Biblical allusions in *Godot*. Faith and hope are intimately connected in this work. Instead of "Philosopher Kings" we have "Philosopher Bums," the two *clochards* who symbolize modern man's condition of being uprooted. In a recent conversation between the American playwright John Guare and director Mike Nichols, who was rehearsing his production of *Godot* (Fall 1988), a couple of important points were made about Beckett's two characters. Guare inquired: "In directing the play, do you have to find your own narrative for it? People say it's about two resistance fighters in the Lot valley. Philip Roth says it's about any day in the life of a writer." Nichols' answer was circuitous but made its point: "With a Chekhov play, if you're specific about the lives of these characters in Russia— if you get it right—then those specifics apply to all our lives. But *Godot* doesn't say it's any specific place, and all the little crutches for character and actor are removed. . . . The work does sustain you. It makes you happy. . . . It's thrilling to see the truth."[27]

Truth is indeed what we sense in all of Beckett's *oeuvre*. But with *Godot* we feel that we are peering into the depths of the writer's own soul. Beckett identified with Didi and Gogo (perhaps more than Didi, the thinker, the tender, nurturing intellectual who protects his earthy, childlike friend). Like the two companions, he was a man on the run, a man without the shelter of a permanent home. This was a time when everyone had to bear the same cross. The cruciform action on *Godot's* stage bears this out. Thus when the clowns Gogo and Didi compare themselves to Christ, Beckett is not being ironic. As G. S. Fraser wrote in *The Times Literary Supplement* (February 10, 1956): "the ambiguity of their attitude toward Godot, their mingled hope and fear, the doubtful tone of the boy's message, represent the state of tension and uncertainty in which the average Christian must live in the world, avoiding presumption, and also avoiding despair." Hélène Baldwin calls Gogo and Didi "the good thief," for they are "attentive to the Lord, they are waiting on God by the foot of the Tree of the Cross."[22]

At the beginning of Act I, Vladimir and Estragon speak of the two thieves, debating the various versions of Christ's death in the Gospels:

VLADIMIR: Do you remember the Gospels?
ESTRAGON: I remember the maps of the Holy Land. Coloured they
    were. Very pretty. The Dead Sea was pale blue. The very look of
    it made me thirsty. That's where we'll go I used to say, that's where
    we'll go for our honeymoon. We'll swim. We'll be happy.
VLADIMIR: You should have been a poet.

ESTRAGON: I was. (Gesturing toward his rags). Isn't that obvious?

. . .

VLADIMIR: The two thieves. Do you remember the story?
ESTRAGON: No.
VLADIMIR: Shall I tell it to you?
ESTRAGON: No.
VLADIMIR: It'll pass the time . . . [23]

Vladimir proceeds to tell that one of the thieves was damned, the other saved. However, he wonders why the Four Evangelists could not agree on a single version. Only one, St. Luke, speaks of a thief being saved, yet "it's the only version [people] know."[24] Neither St. John nor St. Matthew mention any thieves, while St. Mark says that both thieves reviled Christ. It is interesting to note that Beckett changed the "reviled" of the King James version to the more colloquial "abused." In the original French version, he made use of a vulgar, powerful colloquialism: "engueulé ("bawled him out").

Beckett is using the passion narrative to make his point about justice—human and divine—in the way the narrative itself, when it was produced, made use of former prototypes. The pre-Christian text of the Apocrypha, "The Wisdom of Solomon," deals with the treatment of the righteous by the wicked. The wicked oppress the righteous man because he is "inconvenient to them," because he professes to have knowledge of God and calls himself the child of the Lord. The ways of the righteous man are strange. He boasts that God is his father, and so the wicked put him to a test by insult and torture, condemning him finally to a shameful end. Psalm 22 is full of references that anticipate the Scriptures:

All they that see me laugh me to scorn: they shoot out the lip, they shake the head saying
He trusted in the Lord that he would deliver him: let him deliver him, seeing he delighted in him.

. . .

The assembly of the wicked have enclosed me: they pierced my hands and my feet.

The newness of a story lies in the way in which it is not only told, but retold. This is what constitutes the arresting quality of the Passion narrative. In his own manner, Beckett is retelling the same story, but he uses a tenderly ironic approach as he focuses on those humble men who surrounded Christ, those who have their "little cross"[25] to bear, as Didi says.

*   *   *

In his *Philosophies of India*, Heinrich Zimmer states: "Symbols hold the mind to truth but are not themselves the truth, hence it is delusory to borrow them. Each civilization, every age, must bring forth its own . . . . We cannot borrow God. We must suffer his new incarnation from within ourselves. Divinity must descend, somehow, into the matter of our own substance and participate in this peculiar life–process."[26]

In *Waiting for Godot*, Beckett has written a myth for our time. In a note written for *The New Theater Review*, Arthur Miller admits to not understanding or appreciating *Godot* in the mid–1950s, when he himself was under attack by the extreme Right. Later, "when it seemed that the Republic would survive for the time being," he began to laugh at the vaudeville absurdities of the play. He appreciated what he calls "the exuberance of his despair." As in vaudeville, every bit of stage business held out the possibility of some superhuman equilibrium. Miller writes: "The opening of every act raised hope for a miracle—that one might live forever on this small crest of anticipation, and that the lights in the theater would never go on again to force one back into the pawky daylight of the street."[27]

As a reader, and as a writer, Arthur Miller is not at home with subtext. Because Beckett lives in many languages and various cultures, his subtext is a tapestry woven of numerous strands: The Book of Job, the Psalms, Proverbs, the Passion narrative, Gnostic thought, St. Augustine, Dante, the Book of Common Prayer, Pascal's *Pensées*, Nietzsche, Kierkegaard, Wittgenstein. The text itself is haunted by intertextual references, quotations from the French and British poets Beckett studied and taught. The game of literary identification is constantly going on, in the text, between the protagonists of a play, or as a riddle of the questioning, questing mind and failing memory. Echoes from Proust and Joyce abound, but they are only the tip of the iceberg. One recognizes Shakespeare, Lamartine, Baudelaire, Shelley. Most of the time, the quotation is left unfinished, or has a vital part missing, but it reveals that the character lives in the world of literature, that these literary references constitute his or her own structure and being.

In *Godot*, the myth of Christ's Passion and the punishment of Ahasuerus, who refused to alleviate even for a moment Christ's suffering, intersect. Beckett seems to suggest that we are all sufferers like Christ, and Job, and all sinners, atoning wanderers, like Ahasuerus. These intersecting lines also pass through James Joyce's *Ulysses*. As Harold Fisch points out in his book, *The Dual Image: The Figure of the Jew in English and American Literature,* "Gogo and Didi are the heirs of Leopold Bloom."[28]

Joyce's Jewish anti–hero, or comic Odysseus, is a clown. As such he arouses in the reader the traditional comic response associated with the image of the Jew in earlier literature. He is helpless, absurd, as he tries to make some sense of a hostile world. Fisch points out that *Ulysses* is the first major novel in which the Jew functions as a symbol of a universal condition, that of alienation, which has become the reigning myth of our century. Bloom, a kind of Everyman, is a victim, an impotent lover, a cuckolded husband, a dreamer, and most of all a frustrated wanderer. He is unaccommodated man. As a self-exiled writer, living in Zürich, Trieste, Paris, Joyce had a particular insight into the situation of estrangement and rootlessness. Although Bloom is said to have been patterned on a Dublin Jew called Hunter, and on Joyce's literary friend in Trieste, Svevo, he also reflects the novelist's feelings about himself.

As to Beckett, we know that he was Joyce's close young friend, although not his secretary as has been falsely claimed. If the myth of the Jew pervades the subtext of *Waiting for Godot,* it has something to do with the way it was used by Joyce to express the human situation. In Joyce and Beckett, the Jew becomes a symbol of the struggle of the human spirit, perhaps because more than any other group those who were called to witness the work of God were put in a position to bear witness to the boundless cruelty of man.

Most Beckett critics have dimissed, or simply disregarded any mythical aspect of Beckett's thinking, just as they swept aside his political commitments. It is important to begin correcting this lacuna without going overboard to declare that Beckett is a religious writer. Perhaps fertile ground can be found along the careful path of Hélène Baldwin, who states that "attention must be paid to the religious language and to the mysticism which seems to be inherent in much of the work."[29] More than anything else, it is a matter of tone, one penetrated with what Dr. Baldwin calls "dreamy longing or lyrical yearning."[30]

For anyone who has the great privilege of having met Samuel Beckett, the salient feature one recalls is the ever–present sense of humor. It is humor, rather than wit, which means that there is nothing sarcastic about his laughter, that when he laughs it is never to mock, to deride, to criticize, to destroy. Humor always includes the one who laughs in the laughter, one laughs not at others, or their plight, but at oneself, and at the basic absurdity of the human condition. Beckett's laugh is a grimace between merriment and mute sobbing. In his novel *Watt,* Beckett arrives at various gradations of the comic, much as

Baudelaire did in his theoretical essay, "De l'essence du rire." Beckett lists categories of the comic, until he tops them all with what he calls "the mirthless laugh . . . the laugh of laughs, the *risus purus*, the laugh laughing at the laugh, the beholding, the saluting of the highest joke."[31] What is this highest joke? Could it not be the one played by the gods upon the human race.

Like Aeschylus in his *Prometheus*, Beckett shows that we are all victims of cruel divinities who have tied us to the rock of endless pain. It is the fate of humanity to suffer, to endure, to wait for the end—their personal end, not the end of pain since that one is endless. Beckett's message is the same as that of the great classical writers. Like them, this modern classicist is not a pessimist, for a true pessimist does not lift pen to paper. Numerous critics have spoken of his sarcastic irony, his nihilistic view of the world, his despair. This is a reductionist view, one that does not probe the depths of the poet–philosopher.

This is not to say Beckett fails to see the absurdities of life. He does; but his absurdity is that of Kierkegaard. Gogo and Didi might well be two of the Kierkegaardian Knights of Infinite Resignation. There is no reason for them to believe that God is love, but by virtue of an absurd faith—to use the philosopher's own terminology—they still believe in something, at least in waiting. In *Fear and Trembling*, Kierkegaard writes that there is peace and rest in infinite resignation.[32] Didi expresses the same concept when he says:

> We are blessed in this that we happen to know the answer. Yes, in this immense confusion one thing alone is clear. We are waiting for Godot to come. . . . Or for night to fall. We have kept our appointment and that's an end to that. We are not saints, but we have kept our appointment. How many people can boast as much.[33]

We might do well at this point to recall that in his *Journals and Papers*, Kierkegaard wrote: "The present time is the time of despair, the time of the Wandering Jew."[34]

There is a direct allusion to Kierkegaard's best known work in *Godot*. Pozzo, who is one of the princes of this world, objects to the line of questioning of the two bums: "A question A moment ago you were calling me Sir, in fear and trembling, now you're asking me questions. NO good will come of it."[35] If Gogo and Didi are connected to one another by caring and sharing, Pozzo and Lucky's tie is a rope which expresses, in visual terms, the interdependence of a tyrannical master and his dehumanized slave.

When the second couple first appears in Act I, Pozzo is driving Lucky by means of this rope, tied round the "knook's"[36] neck. Lucky enters first, panting and slavering, half choked.

The rope stretches across the length of the stage. Lucky carries all of Pozzo's possessions: his folding camp chair, the picnic basket. Finally Pozzo appears, cracking a whip like a lion tamer. The master jerks on the rope; Lucky falls. Just before this horrifying appearance, Estragon has been questioning Didi about whether they were "tied to Godot." Vladimir answered: "Tied to Godot! What an idea! No question of it. For the moment."[31] Clearly, the two companions' waiting is an exercise of free will. Perhaps the only tie, or connection, might be the invisible one of an ancient covenant. But it is also possible that the covenant lies still in the future since Didi says: "I'm curious to hear what he has to offer. Then we'll take it or leave it."[38]

Pozzo is briefly mistaken for Godot by Gogo, but he soon shows his true mettle. He roars that he is a human being, like the two friends, of the same species, made in God's image. This is a particularly funny line when you see the pretentious man and the two bums side by side. Pozzo does not believe for a moment what he is saying, but he is spouting these mock–religious clichés with venom. This Pozzo, or Bozzo (a big boss who is looking for the Board, as he proclaims in Act II), is on his way to the fair where he threatens to sell his devoted slave. He is a caricature of the Wandering Jew. Indeed he is unable to stop, to rest, except on the folding stool Lucky opens for him. His hell is to keep on moving.

As to the two friends, although they move constantly it is always in circles, not far from the tree where they believe they are to meet Godot. Bare in Act I, the lone tree sprouts some meager leaves for Act II, as if to indicate a possible passage of time, a feeble renewal of life.

Although the tree, as a symbol, exists in every mythology, it is associated in the Judeo-Christian culture with two trees which stood in the middle of the Garden of Eden where God walked in the cool of the evening conversing with Adam and admiring his creation: It is revealing to note than when Pozzo asks Estragon his name, the immediate reply—in the English version—is "Adam."[39] The tree in *Godot* is so weak and crooked that it must be seen as the pale shadow of the two Edenic trees, but its presence is nevertheless interpreted as a sign. It is also identified with the willow. Its leafless state would indicate that all tears have dried up. Still, when the two friends evoke the sound of dead voices whispering, rustling, murmuring, they compare these sounds to that made by leaves. In a passage which parodies the ancient Greek chorus they intone:

VLADIMIR: They make a noise like feathers.
ESTRAGON: Like leaves.
VLADIMIR: Like ashes.
ESTRAGON: like leaves.[40]

Estragon, the former poet, uses a simile from the world of nature, the gardens and woods he remembers. Vladimir, the philosopher and Bible scholar, equates the dead with their final state (ashes to ashes). Yet, since the word ashes follows a metonymic simile ("like feathers," meaning like birds), we do not envision these ashes as lying on or in the ground, but as flying up, making a hissing noise as they rise toward the heavens. These flying ashes might well be those that obscured the sky as they rose through the chimneys of the crematoria.

It is not easy to retain hope when harboring this apprehension. At the start of the play, Vladimir quotes from chapter 13 of *Proverbs*, but the quotation has a few telling lacunae: "Hope deferred maketh the something sick, who said that?" The missing word is "heart." The second part of the proverb is also forgotten: " . . . but when the desire cometh it is the tree of life?" Is there still room for the heart in our pitiless world? One cannot even remember the word. In most ways, Gogo and Didi are also beyond desire, beyond the flickering hope that would stir the heart were this organ still acknowledged. The companion's tree of life is frail, sickly. For a brief instant they contemplate hanging themselves from its pliant branches, then give up the thought, not because they fear for their immortal souls, but because, being practical, they realize that if the lighter one of the two were to succeed in this enterprise, the other one would be left alone. Although they often speak of parting, it is clear that they will remain together. Didi's "little cross" is his friend Gogo, yet he does not wish to part from him. Didi may have forgotten the word "heart," but he is a feeling person, a loyal friend. He and Gogo have been together for fifty years, shared many experiences. They harvested grapes in the Macon country (a rich wine region in France), although they refer to it as the "Cackon"[41] country in one of their numerous scatological jokes. Gogo, it seems, tried to drown himself in the Rhone river, but Didi pulled him out. When in Act II, Didi suggests that perhaps they might be better off apart, Gogo retorts with cruelty: "You say that and you always come crawling back."[42] They often sound like an old married couple.

A tragic note is struck when Gogo states that it would be better if Didi were to kill him, "like the other."[43] Since the two companions have been rehashing the Passion narrative the reference is clear. All the more so since Gogo has also stated that all his life he compared himself to Christ. However, Vladimir still questions in mock-disbelief: "What other?" Estragon/Levi answers: "Like billions of others."[44] Although the retort is tossed off, it lingers in the mind. The image of the war, of so many absurd, endless wars, of concentration and slave labor camps, of penal colonies and torture cells, of block houses and crematoria rise before our eyes. They drive us to despair, fill us with horror and pity. Beckett wants us to be united by this awareness, and this sorrow. But he is also a philosopher–poet who must have read in Kierkegaard's *Sickness unto Death* the following statement:

> Despair is the advantage man has over the beast. And this advantage distinguishes man more than his erect posture, for it implies the infinite erectness and loftiness of being spirit.[45]

Thus, though Beckett's Gogo and Didi are crawlers in the mud, the slime of life, they also "come in on their hands and knees," as Vladimir says. They are suppliants, men of faith who wait on the road for the possible arrival of the spirit. Perhaps they wait simply because this waiting, in itself, is the only dignified attitude of human beings. As to this road, which seems to run through a desert, might it not be the highway of the wayfaring men who "though fools shall not err therein?" It is "the way of holiness" described by Isaiah.

In *Waiting for Godot* Beckett invites all wanderers, all uprooted, exiled, estranged, alienated people, all Wandering Jews—and in this sense perhaps it can be said that all men of our time are like the Jewish people—to stand side by side, shoulder to shoulder, upon this stretch of road, like Gogo and Didi, feeling the warmth of another human being passing into their bodies, waiting with modest but unshakable hope, making of this expectation the very miracle.

NOTES

1. Samuel Beckett, *Waiting for Godot*. New York: Grove Press, 1954, p. 42.

2. *Ibid.*

3. Conversation between Samuel Beckett and the author of this essay in Paris on May 20, 1983.

4. *Ibid.*

5. Alfred Simon, *Beckett*. Paris: Pierre Belfond, 1983, pp. 28–29. Translated from the French by the author of this essay.

6. Sigmund Freud, "The Uncanny" in *The Complete Psychological Works of Sigmund Freud*. Translated and edited by James Strachey *et al.* Vol. XVII (1917–1919). London: The Hogarth Press, 1955, p. 226.

7. *Godot*, p. 39.

8. *Ibid.*, p. 7.

9. *Ibid.*, p. 8.

10. *Ibid.*

11. *Ibid.*, pp. 36, 61. It is interesting to note that in Act I it is Vladimir who says: "Yes, let's go" at the end, while Act II ends with Estragon echoing the very same words. In both cases the two friends remain motionless.

12. *Ibid.*, p. 43.

13. *Ibid.*, p. 8.

14. *Ibid.*, p. 12.

15. *Ibid.*, p. 10.

16. *Ibid.*, p. 16.

17. Hélène Baldwin, *Samuel Beckett's Real Silence.* University Park: Pennsylvania State University, 1980, p. 107.

18. Conversation between Samuel Beckett and the author of this essay in Paris, on May 20, 1983.

19. *Ibid.*

20. Alphonse de Lamartine. Note by the poet to his poem "L'Immortalité."

21. "Never Neglect the Little Things of Life," A Conversation between Mike Nichols and John Guare, *The New Theater Review* (A Lincoln Center Theater Publication), New York, Vol. 1, No. 4: "Samuel Beckett," pp. 3–4.

22. *Samuel Beckett's Real Silence*, p. 122.

23. *Godot*, pp. 8–9.

24. *Ibid.*, p. 9.

25. *Ibid.*, p. 40.

26. Quoted by Joseph Campbell, *The Masks of God, Creative Mythology.* New York: Viking Press, 1968, p. 626.

27. "A Note from Arthur Miller," *The New Theater Review*, Vol. 1, No. 4, p. 2.

28. Harold Fisch, *The Dual Image: The Figure of the Jew in English and American Literature.* London: World Jewish Library, 1971, p. 84.

29. *Samuel Beckett's Real Silence*, p. 5.

30. *Ibid.*, p. 155. "A yearning for something more, something grander."

31. Samuel Beckett, *Watt.* New York: Grove Press, 1959, p. 48.

32. Soren Kierkegaard, *Fear and Trembling/The Sickness Unto Death.* Translated with an Introduction and Notes by Walter Lowrie. Garden City, N.Y.: Doubleday, 1955. On p. 57, Kierkegaard writes: "The infinite resignation is the last stage prior to faith, so that one who has not made this movement has no faith." On p. 62, he adds: "What every man can do is to make the movement of infinite resignation."

33. *Godot*, p. 51.

34. Soren Kierkegaard, *Journals and Papers.* Edited and translated by Howard V. Hong and Edna H. Hong, Bloomington, Ind. and London: Indiana University Press, 1970, p. 37.

35. *Godot*, p. 20.

36. *Ibid.*, p. 23.

37. *Ibid.*, p. 14.

38. *Ibid.*, p. 12.

39. *Ibid.,* p. 25.
40. *Ibid.,* p. 40.
41. *Ibid.*
42. *Ibid.,* p. 38.
43. *Ibid.,* p. 40.
44. *Ibid.*
45. *The Sickness Unto Death,* p. 148.

German-Jewish Writers on the Eve of the Holocaust

Diane R. Spielmann

Elie Wiesel has indicated that the Holocaust and the formation of the State of Israel have spurred on a rethinking of the concept of Judaism.[1] Likewise, the period directly before the Holocaust has taken on a special significance and therefore must be reevaluated.

One area deserving focus is the literature of that period, especially that by German-Jewish writers. Their numbers are overwhelming. To individually name them would literally fill volumes. Indeed, in his lengthy 1934 essay, *Bilanz der deutschen Judenheit* (appearing in English in 1937 as *Insulted and Exiled*), Arnold Zweig, himself a playwright and novelist, devoted an entire chapter to the mere listing of these names. Among the list can be found the names of such acclaimed writers as Arthur Schnitzler, Richard Beer-Hofmann, Franz Kafka, Ernst Toller, Stefan Zweig, Lion Feuchtwanger, Martin Buber, as well as lesser known artists such as Leopold Schwarzschild, Julius Bab, and Ernst Weiss.

The literary field is one among many in which Jews distinguished themselves. Zweig's *Bilanz* provides long lists of German-Jews in virtually every field. However, it is the writer who represents the heartbeat of society. Zweig illuminated this idea in an earlier essay, "Juedischer Ausdruckswille" (The Jewish Will of Expression), published in 1933. He stated that the artist is the bearer as well as the vent of expression. He reveals the burdens, the limitations, the yearning, the doubts and the hopes of the society of which he is an integral part.[2] And according to Sol Liptzin, writers are the most "sensitive spirits" of society, and in Nazi Germany, they were most directly affected.[3]

Writers, as representatives of their society, become a key in trying to understand the milieu of the enlightened, and for the most part assimilated, German-Jew prior to the Holocaust. Within this framework,

Leon Botstein's introduction to a revival of *Stefan Zweig Jewish Legends* offers an interesting observation concerning Holocaust studies and research. Botstein states that generally the focus has been on the destruction of the Eastern European Jewish community. However, looking at the literature of the German-Jewish writer, according to him, "is an almost harrowing journey back . . . to a different Jewish world that Hitler also destroyed, an affluent middle class and assimilated community."[5] He continues, "its traditions and conceits trigger less sympathy; its faith in the power of language, reason, and culture . . . render its members not facile objects of compassion, but a forgotten milieu inspiring ambivalence and discomfort."[6]

As Botstein so aptly pointed out, German-Jews indeed have inspired ambivalence, even among themselves. This was especially true of writers whose very profession depended upon the use of the German language with which they identified. In his essay on nationalism, entitled "Nationalismus und Judentum" (Nationalism and Jewry), published in 1933 in a volume, *Die Aufgabe des Judentums* (The Task of Jewry), which included Zweig's above-mentioned essay, Lion Feuchtwanger outlined four distinct criteria by which to determine nationality. By far the most important of these was language.[7] According to Feuchtwanger, "The individual develops in a language, and does not become free from its bounds his life long. This language thinks for him, categorizes all manifestations of this world, defines them, forms them."[8] As for his own relationship to the German language, Feuchtwanger states, "The German language is the fundamental element of my life's work. As a writer, I live in every respect naturally and ideally from language. . . . I feel myself totally tied to German culture and the German language, and I would not know how I would live without the Germany of this language and culture."[9]

But as fate had it, Lion Feuchtwanger did have to live without the Germany of that language and that culture. Feuchtwanger embarked on a lecture tour abroad in the winter of 1932–33—never to return to his homeland. Henceforth, his life would be one of exile, including a period of internment in a French concentration camp. And it was only through the intervention of Eleanor Roosevelt that Feuchtwanger was able to settle in the United States, where he died in 1958.

The situation of the German-Jewish writer at the beginning of the twentieth century, while not so perilous, was equally as ambivalent because of ever-present anti-Semitic forces. Therefore, any appropriate historical evaluation of German-Jewish writers prior to the Holocaust should begin there.

An argument can be made that the pre-World War I Jewish intellectual community was most influential in Austria, particularly in the coffee houses of Vienna. This intellectual scene would not move to Berlin until after the Armistice. The writers in this Viennese group included Arthur Schnitzler, Richard Beer-Hofmann, Hugo von Hofmannsthal, Karl Kraus, and the German-born Jakob Wassermann.

For this explanation, the works of Arthur Schnitzler will serve as a starting point. Schnitzler, a physician as well as an accomplished writer, was born in Vienna in 1862 and died there in 1931. Although he would never see the National Socialists' rise to power, he nevertheless felt the tension as a Jew and as a writer of German in an anti-Semitic society. He was a youth during the Tiszaeszlár affair, in which the Jewish community of that town within the Austro-Hungarian empire was accused of ritual murder, and he was a young man when Karl Lueger, due primarily to his anti-Semitic political platform, became Mayor of Vienna. As a result, Schnitzler, who is known as one of the most astute commentators and observers of turn-of-the-century Vienna, spent much of his energies as a writer probing his anti-Semitic world.[10]

In the afterword to his 1912 autobiography, *Jugend in Wien* (Youth in Vienna), which he had begun in 1901, Schnitzler reflects on the inordinate amount of attention he has given to anti-Semitism. In this appendix, entitled "Autobiographische Notizen" (Autobiographical Notes), Schnitzler stated, "Throughout these pages there is much talk of Judaism and anti-Semitism, perhaps more so than good taste would warrant . . . however, in the future . . . one will hardly be able to imagine the emotional and spiritual impact (even more than the political or social one) of the Jewish question at the time I have written these lines."[11] Schnitzler ended with a stark analogy, reflecting his medical background. "To remain unaffected [by this issue] was as impossible as a person, who even though anesthesized, can remain objective when he must watch with his very own eyes, as [the surgeon] pierces his body with impure knives, yes—cutting so deeply to the point of drawing blood."[12]

Schnitzler's writings concerning awareness of Judaism to a large extent derive from viewing it in reaction to anti-Semitism. As early as 1900, Schnitzler wrote to the literary critic Georg Brandes, "It will be virtually impossible to write something Viennese in which anti-Semitism does not play a role."[13] Two of Schnitzler's major works deal almost exclusively with his contemporary Jewish society and anti-Semitism. They are the drama *Professor Bernhardi*, completed in 1912, and *Der Weg ins Freie* (The Road to Freedom), a lengthy novel, written in 1908.

Der Weg ins Freie, which Schnitzler called his "most personal and best work" to date,[14] depicts the many different views of contemporary

Jewry in regard to anti-Semitism, assimilation, and the growing Zionist movement. The Jewish society and its varying views are given expression in social gatherings of the community, primarily in the home of Solomon Ehrenberg, a well-to-do merchant. As the host to many of these informal meetings, Ehrenberg is most vocal. He generally introduces the topics concerning Jews living in Vienna. In this regard he contends that Jews are not wholly accepted in society, nor will they ever be. For example, in a discussion with a Jewish socialist, Ehrenberg says,

> I am perhaps a layman in political matters, but I assure you . . . the same thing will occur to you Jewish Social democrats as had occurred to the Jewish Liberals and German nationals. . . . Who created the liberal movement in Austria? . . . the Jews! . . . By whom were the Jews betrayed and abandoned? By the Liberals. Who created the German national movement in Austria? The Jews. By whom were they deserted? . . . what am I saying deserted . . . [more appropriately I should say] spat upon like dogs . . . by the Germans. And similarly it will happen to you in regard to Socialism and Communism. When the soup is finally being served, you will be driven from the table. This has always been the case and will continue to be so.[15]

This straightforward statement by Ehrenberg is not only universal, but has become prophetic in retrospect.

Ehrenberg, however, is a minor character who merely sets the stage for further reflections on the issues he presents. The thoughts he introduces are expounded upon by another character, Heinrich Bermann, who most closely represents Schnitzler himself.[16] Like Schnitzler, Bermann is a writer who is ambivalent about his own Jewish identity. A juxtaposition of a statement by Ehrenberg with one by Bermann will illuminate the difference in the depth of thinking of the respective characters. This is Schnitzler's methodology in reflecting the inner conflicts and ambivalence especially felt by the writer. On the question of Jewish identity in their society, Ehrenberg says forthrightly to an advocate of complete assimilation:

> When someone knocks off your hat while strolling on the *Ringstrasse* because, pardon me when I say so, you have a somewhat Jewish-looking nose, then you will feel Jewish; you can depend on it.[17]

Bermann, however, is reflective:

> At times, one really feels at home in spite of everything, yes, even more so than someone whose family has been here for centuries. It

seems that the mere consciousness of the issue cancels the feeling of alienation, and is simultaneously full of pride, assimilation, and sensitivity.[18]

In this reflective manner, Heinrich Bermann, the writer and main Jewish protagonist of the novel, continues to discuss these issues against the background of the growing Zionist movement. The debates are primarily between himself, at best an ambivalent proponent of assimilation, and Leo, a proponent of Zionism. A neutral observer is a non-Jewish character, Georg, who listens to these debates, and Schnitzler was sure to indicate that no one can be totally objective or neutral on the mingling of Jew and Gentile: there will always be distrust between them.[19] Georg nevertheless begins to appreciate the complexity of the dilemma facing his Jewish countrymen.

Thus, *Der Weg ins Freie* poses the problems the Jews encounter in a less than friendly environment but provides no answers, not even in Zionism.

In contrast, *Professor Bernhardi*, completed four years later in 1912, revolves around a specific situation in which the baseness of anti-Semitism is exposed amid a superficial tolerance. Here, there are no open-ended and intellectualized discussions, but instead a single case in a closed environment which represents a microcosm of the society at large.

Professor Bernhardi, a Jew, is the director of a private medical facility that he helped found. However, his position is vulnerable because of the anti-Semitic factions within the institution. Only one incident is needed to bring the dormant anti-Semitism to the fore.

One of Bernhardi's patients is a terminally ill young woman who nevertheless feels she is fully recovered. In her euphoria, she expects her lover to come for her. Bernhardi does not want to destroy these last moments of happiness for his dying patient. To allow the priest, who has been summoned to the clinic by Ludmilla, the Catholic nurse, to enter the patient's room would do so. Therefore, Bernhardi requests that the priest not enter the room. In the interim, however, Ludmilla does inform the woman of the priest's presence, the shock causes her immediate death, before the priest is able to enter and administer the last sacrament.

Within eight days, the incident is blown out of proportion. Bernhardi is accused of having forcibly blocked the priest's entrance into the patient's room. The future of the institution is thus threatened by the seeming offense to the religious feelings of the Catholic society. With the hope of preventing the dissolution of the facility by the board of trustees and the Austrian Ministry of Education, Bernhardi voluntarily resigns his post in favor of the deputy director, a blatant anti-Semite. Bernhardi, who does not want to become embroiled in politics, is willing to make a statement assuring that his actions were motivated not by the desire to injure religious feelings, but by professional ethics. However, anti-Semitic colleagues, as well as his society in general, initiate an investigation of the incident. As the result of a trial, Bernhardi is found guilty of forcibly hindering the priest from fulfilling the last sacrament. He is sentenced to a two-month prison term. After his release, his attorney wants to have a retrial, since Ludmilla, on whose statement Bernhardi was convicted, has admitted to exaggerating the incident. Bernhardi, however, wants no part of this. He merely wants to return to private practice.

Alongside this main plot, there are subplots, which also point to the vulnerable situation of Jewish physicians because of anti-Semitism. While Bernhardi is facing his own career uncertainties, he is visited by a Jewish gynecologist from the provinces, who is threatened with the loss of his position because of the death of a patient that was beyond his control. Another subplot dealing with the Jewish situation is the election of a physician to the post of head of dermatology in the institute. Bernhardi, while still director, must break a tie vote. He chooses the more qualified candidate, who is Jewish, although non-Jewish officials have made it clear that if Bernhardi chooses the other candidate, who is a non-Jew, it may help Bernhardi's case. Bernhardi, however, stands on principle and chooses the Jew.

The plots occuring in *Professor Bernhardi* are grounded in reality. Schnitzler's father, also a physician, was the head of a clinic he helped found. And because of anti-Semitism, Dr. Schnitzler faced many difficulties throughout his career.[20] Despite a semblance of tolerance fostered by the Austrian Constitution of 1867, anti-Semitism was a definite factor for the Jew living in Schnitzler's Vienna, and it is revealed through the mini-society presented in *Professor Bernhardi.*

The play is primarily a character study in which all of those portrayed represent the different types found in society. Among the non-Jews, there are the rabid anti-Semite, the defenders of Bernhardi, those who are indifferent, and those who display latent anti-Semitism. One also finds the interesting category of the converted Jews, and the conflicts those individuals feel in the situation presented. Likewise, the Jewish characters run the gamut from those who recognize the situation for what it is, and therefore staunchly defend Bernhardi, to those who would like to deny it, and thereby indirectly aid in Bernhardi's conviction. But, whatever their position, every Jew feels a sense of insecurity.

The overall situation is best reflected in the interaction of the Jews and Gentiles. Perhaps the most dramatic statement in this regard is the personal encounter of Bernhardi with the priest after Bernhardi's conviction. On that occasion the priest says to Bernhardi,

> I dispute that you denied me entrance into the room of the dying patient merely because of your sense of responsibility. The true reason for your position against me does not lie in your sense of responsibility, nor in your noble feelings of the moment, as you probably imagine, as I had almost begun to believe, but the real reason lies much deeper, in the roots of your very being. Yes, *Herr Professor*, the real reason was—how shall I put it—an antipathy against me—an uncontrollable antipathy—rather a hostility . . . against that which this garb represents for you and your kind.[21]

Through his keen observations, and talents as a writer, Arthur Schnitzler portrayed realistically the ambivalent milieu of Austria during the last days of the empire in which Jews lived under the guise of superficial tolerance that fostered a dormant anti-Semitism.

The Great War and the Austrian government following it did not change matters for its Jewish citizens. Hugo Bettauer, a Jewish writer born in 1872, although not so acclaimed as Schnitzler in literary circles, was known widely as an international journalist; he continued to give expression to their situation. Bettauer chose satire as his means of depicting his milieu, and in light of events to follow, was to become not only prophetic but actually grotesque.

After having worked as a journalist in both Berlin and New York, Bettauer returned to his native Austria. There, in 1918, he covered the anti-Semitic pogroms in Lvov (Lemberg), his father's home town. However, anti-Jewish sentiment was then running high in Vienna as well as the hinterlands of Galicia. For example, it was popular to blame the loss of the Great War on the Jews. Bettauer records that there were widespread calls for *"Hinaus mit den Juden"* ("Out with the Jew").[22] Thus by 1923, he began writing his most famous and popular work, *Die Stadt ohne Juden* (The City Without Jews).

The satirical novel is divided into two sections. The first begins after the successful election of the Christian Socialists who advocated *"Hinaus mit den Juden."* Jews, according to them, have controlled banks, money, industry, and even the coffee houses since 1914. The Austrians who are slower in temperament cannot compete. Therefore, the Christian socialists have set forth a specific program of expulsion which states that Jews will be able to sell their businesses, and then leave. Depending on their professions, the Jews will be given anywhere from three to six months to do so. The death penalty is prescribed for those who would remain in Austria, with the exception of the old and the feeble. Following this declaration, there is a detailed description of "Who is a Jew." In order to offset any economic repercussions following the immediate expulsion of the Jews, world-wide Christendom has promised financial aid to Austria.

In this first section Bettauer examines the lamentations of the Jewish community. He even makes obvious references to such individuals as Arthur Schnitzler.[23] He also depicts the euphoria within the Christian community. Six months hence, after the last Jew had left, church bells chime in celebration, and Section One ends with Mayor Karl Maria Laberl, an obvious reference to Karl Lueger, addressing a crowd, *"Meine lieben Christen"* ("My dear Christians"). With the close of this phrase, an immense rainstorm ensues, which forces the crowd to disperse. In this manner, Bettauer foreshadows the impending downfall economically and culturally of Austria which he describes in detail in Section Two.

This section begins one year after the expulsion. As a result, inflation has become uncontrollable, businesses have failed, Austria has lost her status in the fashion world, and she has become void of any intelligentsia or culture. In this scenario, based heavily on stereotype, Bettauer even includes a chapter on mistresses who yearn for the kind treatment they had received from their Jewish patrons, as opposed to that of their Gentile patrons.

What heightens the satire even further is Bettauer's heavy usage of such Yiddishisms as *Kapores, Ganef,* and *Masseltoff* within the Christian community which indicates the subtle integration of Jewish influence over the years.

Soon the country begins to realize that Austria, whose economy and culture have suffered, cannot continue to survive without Jews. There is an eventual call for another election followed by a turnabout of the laws so that the Jews may return. Thematically, Bettauer accomplishes this by intertwining a subplot in which Leo, a Jewish artist exiled to France by the expulsion laws, has connived his way back into Austria through an ingenious scheme, so that he may be reunited with his Gentile girlfriend, Lotte. Section Two and the novel end as Mayor Laberl, now a Social Democrat, welcomes Leo back with the words, *"Mein lieber Jude"* ("My dear Jew"). All is well that ends well—at least in this satire.

Die Stadt ohne Juden achieved great success and popularity. By the end of 1924, 80,000 copies were sold, and there were more than 250,000 additional copies in translation.[24] The following year it was made into a movie and successfully shown in Vienna and Berlin, but not in New York for fear of injuring sensitivities.[25]

Thus, a program presented as a satire becomes reality a decade later in precisely those countries in whose culture it is depicted. Ironically, Bettauer himself, like Schnitzler before him, never saw the unprecedented brutality of the Holocaust nor the initial rise to power of the National Socialists. In 1925, in reaction to another of his works, involving sexual mores, Bettauer was assassinated by a right-wing fanatic who was acquitted soon after.

The popularity of *Die Stadt ohne Juden* continued, primarily in the German-speaking community. The theme was adopted not in New York, not in Paris, and not in London, but it was adopted in Berlin. Arthur Landsberger, a Berlin-Jewish novelist and editor born in 1876, wrote his version, *Berlin ohne Juden*. As mentioned above, after World War I, the focus and strength of the Jewish intellectual scene shifted from Vienna to Berlin.

Landsberger, born into a well-to-do Berlin Jewish family, was primarily known as a writer of popular adventure stories. He was responsible for German translations of Yiddish works and introduced Jewish themes, especiallay those of Eastern Europe, into German literature. His works included *Das Ghettobuch* (The Ghetto Book), 1914; and *Das Volk des Ghettos* (The People of the Ghetto), 1916. However, his most popular piece was *Berlin ohne Juden* published in 1925, as the Berlin counterpart to Bettauer's *Die Stadt ohne Juden*.

Contrary to his custom, Landsberger began this novel with a preface.[26] After reading Bettauer's book, he felt compelled to do so in order to carry the theme to its logical conclusion in Berlin. In the preface, Landsberger acknowledged that he would no doubt insult various individuals and movements, but this was of no concern to him. He felt that by writing this book he was exercising his patriotic duty. He ended the Preface by calling the novel a tragic satire.[27] By adding the word "tragic" Landsberger has already, in the preface, lent a more serious tone to his work. And this becomes the basis for a literary comparison to the earlier *Stadt ohne Juden*.

Just as Bettauer began his novel by means of a justification for the expulsion laws, so too does Landsberger. As a result of blaming the Great War on the Jews, the German population refers to Jews as "Vermin"; to cite from *Berlin ohne Juden,*

> Within no time the entire economy, in light of the war and poverty, was nothing but the result of the devilish Jews. Jews were the Vermin who nurtured themselves as parasites on the populace. They are bloodsuckers and beasts of prey who deserve to be locked up in cages.[28]

This language is by far more virulent than the language used by Bettauer. Literature does not develop in a vacuum; it is based in reality regardless as to how it is presented. The language that was used in a satire—whether comic or tragic—was commonplace in the society in which and for whom it had been written. It is this continued use of such language in reality, as reflected by the literature, that set the stage for its acceptance, and hence the "logical conclusion" of the Final Solution.

Next, in *Berlin ohne Juden*, Landsberger presents the political platform of expulsion. Unlike Bettauer, he adopts a more serious tone, and devotes more time to the concept of expulsion. In the novel there are lengthy discussions and parliamentary debates on this issue. Proponents argue that it is hardly without historical precedent—but one that has been exercised in almost every European country, most notably in Spain and Portugal. Landsberger provides for the Jewish response to which he allots equal time. Oppenheim, the distinguished representative of the Jewish community, gives historic examples of the downfall of civilizations after the expulsion of their Jews, and by way of contrast he points to successful civilizations into which Jews had been welcomed.

As the program is implemented, in a manner similar to that of *Die Stadt ohne Juden*, there is continued serious handling of the subject. Whereas Bettauer did not even mention the difficulties of resettling a large number of Jewish refugees as a result of the expulsion, Landsberger goes into considerable detail. Plans to absorb the homeless Jews are based upon the ratio of Jewish populations in countries such as the United States, Britain, Scandinavia, France, and even Argentina. Palestine is also included, and her importance is underscored in that she must absorb those Jews who have found no other refuge. Interestingly enough, Landsberger can consider only those nations in which there already are Jews, with Palestine as a last resort. Again, Landsberger's version, even though a satire, is grounded in a bitter sense of reality.

Landsberger, as an additional alternative, raises the specter of suicide which Bettauer barely considers in his work. For those Jews already established and acculturated in Germany, suicide becomes not just a viable, but actually the only alternative. In *Berlin ohne Juden* 96 distinguished members of the Jewish community, including Oppenheim, commit suicide.

After the initial celebrations of music and swastika waving, Berlin without Jews begins its economic and cultural decline. As a result, within a three-year period, the Jews are invited back to Berlin due to the intervention of individuals of the Oppenheim family who are involved in mixed marriages. Jews returning to Berlin number 450,000 of an original 586,000, and as in Bettauer's fiction, "all is well that ends well."

Even though Landsberger's novel is more detailed, it is not as effective as Bettauer's, despite its popularity. The plot Landsberger developed for the initial National Socialist takeover is too convoluted. It involved communist schemes intertwined with those of the fascists. Their respective fictional intrigues only detract from the major focus. Furthermore, the strain of realism employed by Landsberger, and then dropped suddenly for the proverbial happy ending, as the Jews return to Berlin, does not work from the point of view of literature. On the other hand Bettauer, who had established an utterly ridiculous tone from the onset of his "Novel of the Future," as he subtitled it, successfully implemented the equally ridiculous happy ending, and thereby created a much more effective work.

In either case, however, the mere fact that these "fictions" were written and then received with popularity in the German-speaking lands indicates that the tragedy was real and impending. Could there actually have been a happy ending in the minds of either man? Unlike Schnitzler or Bettauer, Landsberger did see the Nazi accession to power. But, as his fictional character Oppenheim did in *Berlin ohne Juden,* Landsberger committed suicide in 1933.

In tracing the Jewish intellectual community from Vienna to Berlin, Landsberger's novel served as a transition for this shift. From 1919 to 1933 the center for Jewish artists writing in German was Berlin. It was the home of such writers as Alfred Doeblin, Kurt Tucholsky, Emil Ludwig, Georg Hermann, Arnold Zweig, and Lion Feuchtwanger.

Arnold Zweig is an example of a German-Jewish writer concerned with Jewish issues during that period. Zweig was born in 1887 in Upper Silesia, and had moved to Munich and then to Berlin by 1923. He was an acclaimed writer having won the Kleist Prize in 1914 for his play *Ritualmord in Ungarn* ("Ritual Murder in Hungary"), based on the Tiszaeszlár affair, and having achieved extensive popularity for his novel of the war, *Der Streit um den Sergeanten Grischa* (*The Case of Sergeant Grischa*). His essays included, "Das ostjuedische Antlitz" (The Face of the Eastern European Jew), 1920; "Caliban," a study of anti-Semitism, 1927; "Juden auf der deutschen Buehne" (Jews on the German Stage), 1928; and the aforementioned "Juedischer Ausdruckswille" (The Jewish Will of Expression), 1933. But perhaps the most powerful essay by Zweig on Jewish issues is *Bilanz der deutschen Judenheit. Die Wahrheit ueber die Deutschen Juden. Ein Versuch,* also mentioned earlier. It was published in 1934 by Querido in the Netherlands, and translated into English by 1937 as *Insulted and*

Exiled. However, an exact translation of the title, "An Account of German-Jewry, The Truth Concerning German Jews, An Attempt," gives a better picture of its content and purpose. It is Zweig's statement and answer as a reaction to the Nazi accession to power.

Written in the fall of 1933, after Zweig had resettled his family in Palestine, *Bilanz* is an accounting of the status and contributions of German Jewry from the Enlightenment to his times. It is not only an attempt to understand what has happened throughout the course of history, and what has gone awry, but also Zweig's personal catharsis in the form of a written justification for Jews in Germany, as well as an outcry against the atrocities he has witnessed. His very dedication takes on the tone of a warning:

For our Ancestors: A Memorium
For our Exiled: A Document
For our Sons: A Reminder
For our Grandsons: An Introspective.[29]

He divides his treatise into three distinct sections: "A Description of Affairs," "A Jewish Segment," and "A Prognosis."

In Section One Zweig, after a brief description of immediate circumstances in Germany, develops a tractate in order to attempt an understanding of the human condition within social development and group psychology.[30] He applies this to the *Fuehrerprinzip* combined with ultra nationalism.[31] Following the war, Jews are blamed for Germany's loss. Zweig enumerates the reasons, based upon stereotypes not necessarily true, why the Jew becomes a convenient scapegoat. The reasoning is, as unarmed inhabitants intertwined in the population, Jews are physically darker, economically powerful, and have their own national identity.[32] Zweig continues that the National Socialists were able to apply this scapegoat theory based upon the foundation established by the "Protocols of the Elders of Zion" and later mis-construed through the Zionist Congress.[33]

Zweig then questions whether Europe can tolerate and accept the insanity of a small number of poorly educated individuals who, with the help of a group of officers and hysterical students, have banded together into an army in order to place themselves in tyrannical possession of a state.[34]

According to Zweig, separating Jews from Germans after a blending together of more than one thousand years is impossible.[35] Jews are no more a separate *Volk* than are Bavarians or Swabians. All of these groups, including Jews, are Germans.[36]

Zweig concludes this section on a somewhat optimistic note. Jews who throughout their history have overcome will do so once more, and it is his hope that Germany will not follow the tide of the Nazis.[37] That turned out, of course, to be a desperate and ultimately futile hope for the year 1933.

Section Two, "A Jewish Segment" is the actual accounting of Jews in German society and culture by means of listing them individually in virtually every field of art, science, business, and politics. As such, this section serves as the justification for Jews in Germany. It is the lengthiest, the most straightforward, and least philosophical section of the book. Zweig merely fills pages upon pages with names, ending each segment with 1933, and the consequent dissolution of a one-time prosperous and mutually beneficial society for both Germans and Jews.

Zweig searches within historical development for reasons for this dissolution. Jews, since the time of Heinrich Heine, have always had a social consciousness, which Zweig considers the key to the development of any society.[38] In Nazi Germany, socialism has been misconstrued. The National Socialists have utilized the term only to attract the masses: in actuality they are not at all socialists.[39] Zweig concludes this section by calling for a social restructuring. It is primarily a failure in the social order that has brought about the insanity of racial theory as applied to the Jews. If it were not directed against the Jews, it would have been directed against another group.[40] In other words, Zweig saw anti-Semitism, not in and unto itself, but as an example in proving the failure of social development. With this, Zweig leads into his third and final section of *Bilanz*.

Section Three, "A Prognosis" is by its very nature the most problematic—the future can be predicted only insofar as one can think through a logical consequence based upon past events. As a result, Section Three is the shortest section, and yet the most philosophical.

Zionism is discussed within this context. German Jews, who have always felt at home in the spirit of internationalism—defined by Zweig as a horizontal development in a social framework—have turned to Zionism as an alternative. It has become necessary for Jews to also develop through a vertical growth or along national lines.[41] As early as 1933 Zweig recognized that annihilation was not an impossibility: "One can have no doubt that the *Voelkischen* would implement expulsion and annihilation of the Jews if they are allowed to do so by the nations of Europe."[42] In a desperate attempt, Zweig appeals to humanity reiterating that Jews have contributed to society, *"Die Menschheit braucht Juden."*[43]

"Humanity Needs Jews" not only for their contributions, but as a measure for social progress within the development of civilization.[44] That which went awry in modern society can be traced back to a subtle flaw during the Emancipation. Jews were accepted "despite their identity," instead of "for their identity."[45]

Zweig concluded his Prognosis and *Bilanz* with the subheading, "The Risk of the Future." The tone is one of disappointment, but not of total resignation. He hoped for the "triumph of wisdom" in the development of a new social order based on an international spirit in which Jews would serve as an example.[46]

Above all, *Bilanz* was a catharsis for Arnold Zweig, the Jew who tried to understand what lead to that which was incomprehensible.

Mentioned earlier for his essay, "Nationalismus und Judentum" (Nationalism and Jewry), Lion Feuchtwanger was a friend and contemporary of Arnold Zweig. Feuchtwanger, a Berlin writer who was born into an Orthodox Jewish family in 1884, was also occupied by Jewish issues throughout his literary career. Known as a historical novelist, Feuchtwanger once commented, "Of the fifteen novels that I wrote, seven are concerned with Jewish subjects."[47]

As a novelist, Feuchtwanger employed past events in order to explore what Berendsohn calls, "the critical moments of Jewish history which have relevance to our own times."[48] His approach differs considerably from his friend Zweig, who was concerned with the same issues. Whereas Zweig, especially in *Bilanz*, had a philosophical tendency for explicit reasoning and exploration into the human psyche, Feuchtwanger acts more as the pure historian who chronicles the events without elaborate philosophizing.

This can be demonstrated by briefly juxtaposing Zweig's *Bilanz*, 1933, with Feuchtwanger's *Der Gelbe Fleck, Die Ausrottung von 500,000 Juden*, 1936 (The Yellow Mark, The Destruction of 500,000 Jews). Both works were written in reaction to the Nazi accession to power. *Bilanz* is an accounting which would appear to be straightforward. However, it is also subtitled "Ein Versuch," (An Attempt). In other words, Zweig, within his chosen title, already has indicated "an attempted" explanation which could lead to the events he had witnessed. As demonstrated above, for this purpose Zweig employed psychology and social theory from which he could deduce that the course of civilization, especially since the Enlightenment, had been flawed, giving rise to the present situation. Zweig even implied that circumstances can possibly be rectified through a new social order. Thus, Zweig not only presented his situation but also tried to find the reasons for it, and even suggested solutions.

In *Der Gelbe Fleck*, Feuchtwanger's approach is much simpler. He presents the events as they are without theorizing. He states in his preface, "This book of the Third Reich compiles in all objectivity, the material which one calls the 'Solution to the Jewish Questions.' "[49] As for the reasons behind the present situation, Feuchtwanger offers no explanation, merely straightforward assessment.

> To a large extent, these bestial events with which [this Pogrom] has occurred are derived from deep-seated hostility toward common sense and understanding; pure insanity; pure joy of brutality; defaming of human value; and degradation of one's neighbor due to hatred.[50]

After the preface, Feuchtwanger proceeds with a factual account beginning just before the Nuremberg Laws through a chapter dealing with Jews in concentration camps, including pages filled with obituaries of prominent Jews. He ends the book with "Das andere Deutschland," (The Other Germany) stating that this study of present-day Germany would not be complete without mentioning the Germans who find the government and its policies odious.[51]

The account here is chronological and factual. Feuchtwanger cites from the available sources and includes photographs. It is his purpose to state events and history as they are so that the reader may make his own deductions, and from that choose his course of action. "History is the struggle of the reasonable minority against the powerful masses of stupidity. The purpose of *Der Gelbe Fleck* is to demonstrate the difficulty of this struggle. This is illustrated by documenting vital material for the historian of all times."[52]

Feuchtwanger was a writer of action, and thus Lothar Kahn entitles his biography of Feuchtwanger *Insight and Action*. Kahn says "Feuchtwanger . . . possessed the audacity 'to say what was' . . . ."[53] "[He] . . . took an active part in opposing the Nazis, making speeches, writing articles, trying to inform and arouse the Germans . . . , " according to his secretary, Hilde Waldo.[54] However, Feuchtwanger's main genre was the novel. And to him history as well as his own experiences could best be expressed in this medium. Art is used for the sake of history, according to Berendsohn in his article on Feuchtwanger.[55]

Two years before *Der Gelbe Fleck*, Feuchtwanger wrote the novel *Die Geschwister Oppenheim* (*The Oppermanns*), which mirrored the experiences of Jews in Germany.[56] According to Kahn, "few writers of the time had a deeper sense of these events, studied them more closely, or experienced them more directly than Feuchtwanger."[57] In direct reference to *Die Geschwister Oppenheim*, Kahn begins his bi-

ography, "my interest in Feuchtwanger was sparked when, as teen-
ager, I read *The Oppermanns*, which depicted better than any book
before or since the insidious machinations of the Nazi regime in its
early months of power."[58]

Die Geschwister Oppenheim begins in Berlin on November 16, 1932,
the fiftieth birthday of the main protagonist, Dr. Gustav Oppenheim,
who is the biographer of Lessing. It concludes with his death in the
summer of 1933 as a result of his internment, under false identification
papers, in Concentration Camp Moosach.

Without adding anything further to that description of start and
finish of the novel, one can immediately make inferences from the
symbolism. The main protagonist has turned fifty, a time when one
takes account of one's life. Gustav is the biographer of Gotthold
Ephraim Lessing, an Enlightenment figure of German literature. As
for the dates of the novel, November 16 is the midst of autumn. The
conclusion is Gustav's death, which takes place in the summer—just
after the year has reached its peak. The concentration camp is the
end-all of the events that began nine months earlier—the time it
takes to form a new life, in this case, Nazi Germany.

The novel, describing conditions in Berlin for the Jews during that
period, depicts the various types: assimilationist, Zionist, professional,
businessman, idealist, and pragmatist. Each representative is to be
found either directly in the Oppenheim family or associated with it.

The Oppenheims are a well-established merchant family, who have
resided in Berlin since the nineteenth century. A chain of furniture
stores is run by Gustav's younger brother, Martin. They have another
brother, Edgar, a laryngologist, as well as a sister, Klara, who is
married to Lavendel, a seemingly successful Eastern European Jewish
businessman. There had also been an older brother, Ludwig, who
was killed during the Great War. With the exception of Gustav, each
Oppenheim sibling has a family. In total they represent a typical
Berlin Jewish family in 1933.

Tracing the family from its strong beginnings of Immanuel Oppenheim, founder of the furniture business, through to the fate of all
of its family members including the youngest generation, the novel
presents the disintegration of the family as a result of the Nazi regime.
With its decay in its structure, *Die Geschwister Oppenheim* is similar
to Thomas Mann's novel *Buddenbrooks*. The difference, however, is
obvious. Unlike the Buddenbrooks, whose decay is internal, the
Oppenheims are a strong family, and would have continued as such
were it not for the Nazi government.

In its methodology, *Die Geschwister Oppenheim* is reminiscent of Schnitzler's *Der Weg ins Freie*. Arthur Schnitzler, as we have seen, depicted the different Jewish types in Vienna—the assimilationist, the Zionist, the writer idealist, the pragmatist. And just as Schnitzler, Feuchtwanger expressed their respective ideas in the various gatherings of these individuals. In *Der Weg ins Freie* the individuals involved were members of a particular Viennese-Jewish society, in *Die Geschwister Oppenheim* the individuals involved were members of a particular Berlin-Jewish family.

The sense of urgency, however, because of the obvious political circumstance, is much greater in Feuchtwanger's portrayal. As a result, the open-endedness, as the title indicates, and as previously discussed, cannot be ascribed to *Die Geschwister Oppenheim*. That would have been impossible in Hitler's Germany.

The various members of the Family Oppenheim must take action in order to secure their fate or face death as did the 17-year-old Berthold, Martin's son. He in many ways more closely resembled his uncle Gustav, who also perished in part because of his ideals. Unable to compromise the truth in face of a National Socialist teacher, Berthold committed suicide. Gustav's death following his internment in a concentration camp was also the result of his quest for truth. He had returned to Germany from safety in exile under false identification papers and was therefore incarcerated. Juxtaposed to these idealists are Lavendel, the pragmatist who, even before the Nazi takeover, had acquired American citizenship for himself and his family, and Ruth, the 17-year-old daughter of the physician Edgar Oppenheim. During the many family gatherings, it was Ruth, the young Zionist, who ridiculed her elders for procrastinating action in light of an uncertain future. She had made plans for resettlement to Palestine.

The complete dissolution of the family is represented in the dispersion of each of these family members. After Ruth has immigrated to Palestine, her father takes his medical practice to Paris. Martin, after his son's suicide, reestablishes himself in London. With the end of the novel, the once strong Oppenheims are either dead or scattered throughout the world—an ominous foreboding for the fate of European Jewry. Feuchtwanger presented this warning throughout the novel, especially with a citation from the Talmud which for him represented the coming fate of German-Jewry.

"It is not ordained to reap what you have sown."[59]

Feuchtwanger also commented on the immediate future of Nazi Germany, in which all values were distorted and turned about. He

portrayed this most succinctly with Gustav's observations while in
Concentration Camp Moosach,

> [In this work group] there were twenty-four inmates, most of whom
> were intellectuals, professors, physicians, authors, and attorneys. They
> were being instructed [according to the Laws set down in *Mein Kampf.*]
> And who was the one doing the instructing to these learned men?—
> none other than an inexperienced peasant boy.[60]

Thus the prophetic eyes of Lion Feuchtwanger evaluated National
Socialism in 1933.

As a professional group, writers were the quickest to react to the
National Socialist accession to power. This group included non-Jewish
as well as Jewish men and women of letters. Most left Germany
within the first two years, many immediately after the formation of
the Hitler government. Literature in Exile groups were founded, among
them, the PEN Club and the *Aufbau* newspaper, the latter having an
international readership to this day.

The swift reaction by the writing profession can be attributed to
two very basic reasons. Traditionally, writers as a group are one of
the most sensitive to trends in a society. Also, by definition, a writer
depends on language, and language, as argued by Lion Feuchtwanger
in *Nationalismus and Judentum*, more than any other characteristic,
defines a national entity. Thus, in the Third Reich, writers, by the
very nature of their profession, were without a country.

Even though many non-Jewish writers left Germany voluntarily,
there is a very important distinction between them and their Jewish
colleagues. In the words of Elie Wiesel, "Not every victim was a Jew,
but every Jew was a victim." This phrase, so poignantly coined by
Wiesel, contains the key to understanding the situation of the Jew in
Europe. Not only was there the obvious immediate physical danger
borne out by the eventual mass extermination, but there was also a
profound psychological effect, especially in the years preceding what
was to become the Holocaust.

Non-Jewish writers who were anti-National Socialist for either
moral or political reasons were not marked for annihilation. If they
chose to remain in Germany, their fate involved concentration camp
and hard labor, but not death. The distinction lies in having a choice.
For Berthold Brecht, for example, who left immediately after the
Reichstag fire of February 1933, or Thomas Mann, it was not morally
possible to remain in Germany and be silent. Nonetheless, they had
a choice. For the Jewish writer, however, there was no choice. They
were forced to leave, or be exterminated.

Because of the writer's dependence upon his language within a nation, many could not bear exile, and thus faced death by their own hand. This group included Ernst Toller, author of *Hinkemann*, who committed suicide in New York in 1939; Stefan Zweig, author of *Die Welt von Gestern* (The World of Yesterday) which in many ways foreshadowed his suicide in Brazil in 1943; Kurt Tucholsky, the Berlin journalist who took his life in Sweden in 1935; and the above-mentioned journalist, author of *Berlin Ohne Juden*, Arthur Landsberger who committed suicide in Berlin as early as 1933.

And then there were those killed in concentration camps. Georg Hermann, the Berlin author of *Jettchen Gebert*, which depicted the developing Jewish petit-bourgeois following the Napoleonic wars, was murdered in Auschwitz in 1943 at the age of 71. Gertrude Kolmar, poet in the style of Nelly Sachs and Else Lasker-Schuler, was murdered in 1943 at the age of 49, camp unknown. Lion Feuchtwanger had also been in a concentration camp. It was through the intervention of Eleanor Roosevelt that he was freed from Gurs, and permitted to enter the United States, settling in California.

Their lives spared, the exiled authors, however, for the most part never felt quite at home in their new environments: Learning a new language at a later stage in life is never an easy task. Feuchtwanger died in 1958 in California, never having become a United States citizen. His good friend Arnold Zweig, who had expressed Zionist ideals as early as 1911 in his autobiographical fiction *Die Familie Klopfer,* immigrated to Palestine in 1933. However, as a Zionist hoping for a Jewish State with international ideals, Zweig was very quickly disappointed by his fellow Zionists. As early as 1936, he began expressing these feelings to Lion Feuchtwanger.[61] Ironically, in 1948, with the establishment of the State of Israel, Arnold Zweig left his home in Haifa, and returned to East Germany, with the hope of finding a socialist utopia there. However, toward the end of his life, Zweig refused East Germany's request to condemn Israel in the aftermath of the Six-Day War. Zweig, who did not find happiness again in his search for a new homeland, is representative for most of his colleagues who were likewise forced into exile.

The situation created by the National Socialists did not occur overnight. The anti-Semitism which lead to death and exile had been festering in the society long before, as illustrated by Schnitzler and, in particular, Bettauer. Neither saw the Nazi rise to power, but both toyed with the idea of leaving their homeland. Moreover, Bettauer ironically and tragically, fell victim to the very sentiment he tried to expose. Murray Hall in his study, *Der Fall Bettauer* (The Bettauer Case) contends that anti-Semitism provided the driving force behind

Bettauer's assassination in 1925 by a right-wing fanatic, as well as the subsequent speedy acquittal of the perpetrator.[62] Furthermore, anti-Semitism was the root of the censorship trial against Bettauer, which had originally drawn the attention of his murderer.[63]

As for Schnitzler, it was only because he was born a generation earlier that he was prevented from facing the fate of the above-mentioned writers who were to follow him. Nevertheless, Schnitzler also recognized the present dangers as well as the dangers to come. As a result, he too grappled with the concept of leaving Austria for Palestine. In his 1908 novel, *Der Weg ins Freie*, Leo the Zionist asks Heinrich Bermann what he will do if there is a return to the *Scheiterhaufen* (the stake). Heinrich, the writer and anti-Zionist who, as mentioned above, represents Schnitzler, responds, "In that case . . . I hereby state emphatically . . . I will become your adherent."[64] There is further evidence in support of Schnitzler having pondered the possibility of being forced to leave his native Austria. In 1942, at the height of the Final Solution, and eleven years after Schnitzler's death, *Aufbau* published an undated letter by Schnitzler entitled "Meine Stellung zum Zionismus" (My Position Toward Zionism). In it he stated that as a "German writer of the Jewish race," his home is in a German-speaking environment. However, he does not totally dismiss Zionism, especially for the suffering Eastern European Jew.[65] Following these words, *Aufbau* editorialized that during Schnitzler's lifetime, these arguments were representative of Central European Jewry for the most part, but given the date of May 1942, Arthur Schnitzler, no doubt, would have changed his views regarding Zionism—even for himself.[66]

Thus, the assessments and reactions by German-Jewish writers to their environment can be seen not only in their works, but also in their very lives, even a generation earlier. The examples given here, beginning with Schnitzler and Bettauer in Vienna, leading to Landsberger as the transition to Berlin, and concluding with Zweig and Feuchtwanger represent but a few of a very large and vocal group. And, in reference to these men and women of letters, and their profession, Arnold Zweig in 1933 in an afterword to his essay, "Juedischer Ausdruckswille," said

> A bullet cannot drive a writer, whom it has hit, into silence because he is a Jew and an unabashed seeker of truth. What has been made into a living word, cannot be struck down dead. On the other side of Might and its bloody prophesies stands the written word.[67]

NOTES

1. Irving Abrahamson, ed., *Against Silence The Voice and Vision of Elie Wiesel*, Vol. I. New York: Holocaust Library, 1985, pp. 251–52.

2. Arnold Zweig, "Juedischer Ausdruckswille," *Die Aufgabe des Judentums*. Paris: Europaeischen Merkur, 1933, p. 55. All translations into English by Diane Spielmann, unless indicated otherwise.

3. Sol Liptzin, *Germany's Stepchildren*. Philadelphia: The Jewish Publication Society of America, 1948, p. 1.

4. Leon Botstein, "Introduction" in *Jewish Legends by Stefan Zweig*. New York, Markus Wiener Publishing, 1987, p. vii.

5. *Ibid.*, p. vii.

6. *Ibid.*, pp. vii–viii.

7. Lion Feuchtwanger, "Nationalismus and Judentum." *Die Aufgabe des Judentums*. Paris: Europaeischen Merkur, 1933, p. 21.

8. *Ibid.*,

9. *Ibid.*, pp. 23–24.

10. Arthur Burkhard, "Schnitzler, Symbol of Austria's Past." *Books Abroad*, Jan. 1930, p. 20.

11. Therese Nickl *and* Heinrich Schnitzler, eds., *Arthur Schnitzler, Jugend in Wien*. Vienna: Fritz Molden, 1968, pp. 328–29.

12. *Ibid.*, p. 329.

13. Kurt Bergel, ed., *Georg Brandes und Arthur Sshnitzler: Ein Briefwwechsel*. Bern: Francke, 1956, p. 83.

14. Therese Nickl *and* Heinrich Schnitzler, eds., *Hugo von Hofmannsthal, Arthur Schnitzler, Briefwechsel*. Bern: Francke, 1956, p. 97.

15. Arthur Schnitzler, "Der Weg ins Freie" in *Die Erzaehlende Schriften*. Frankfurt: S. Fischer, 1962, pp. 696–97.

16. For a further discussion, see Diane R. Spielmann, "Ambivalence in the Works of Arthur Schnitzler Portrayed Through Dilettantism and Through the Jewish Situation." *Doctoral Dissertation*, The City University of New York, 1987, pp. 211, 220.

17. A. Schnitzler, *Der Weg ins Freie*, p. 689.

18. *Ibid.*, pp. 757–58.

19. *Ibid.*, pp. 661, 671.

20. Therese Nickl *and* Heinrich Schnitzler, eds., *Arthur Schnitzler Jugend in Wien: Eine Autobiographie*. Vienna: Fritz Molden, 1968, pp. 199–201.

21. Arthur Schnitzler, "Professor Bernhardi" in *Die dramatischen Werke*, 1. Frankfurt: S. Fischer, 1962, pp. 433–34. Translation into English by Diane Spielmann and Marianne Gilbert.

22. Murray G. Hall, *Der Fall Bettauer*. Vienna: Loecker, 1978, p. 171.

23. Hugo Bettauer, *Die Stadt ohne Juden Ein Roman von Uebermorgen*. Vienna and Leipzig: R. Loewit, 1924, p. 88.

24. Hall, p. 24.

25. *Ibid.*, p. 188.

26. Arthur Landsberger, *Berlin ohne Juden*. Hannover: Paul Steegemann, 1925, p. 7.

27. *Ibid.*, p. 11.

28. *Ibid.*, p. 114.

29. Arnold Zweig, *Bilanz der deutschen Judenheit. Die Wahrheit ueber de Deutschen Juden. Ein Versuch.* Amsterdam: Querido, 1934, p. 3.

30. *Ibid.*, p. 87.

31. *Ibid.*, p. 92.

32. *Ibid.*, p. 96.

33. *Ibid.*, pp. 98–101.

34. *Ibid.*, p. 108.

35. *Ibid.*, p. 118.

36. *Ibid.*, p. 120.

37. *Ibid.*, p. 125.

38. *Ibid.*, p. 274.

39. *Ibid.*, p. 279.

40. *Ibid.*, p. 283.

41. *Ibid.*, p. 307.

42. *Ibid.*, p. 309.

43. *Ibid.*, p. 309.

44. *Ibid.*, p. 313.

45. *Ibid.*

46. *Ibid.*, pp. 313–315.

47. Walter A. Berendsohn, "Lion Feuchtwanger and Judaism" in John M. Spalek, *Lion Feuchtwanger The Man, His Ideas, His Work.* Los Angeles: Hennessey and Ingalls, 1972, p. 27.

48. *Ibid.*, p. 28.

49. Lion Feuchtwanger, *Der Gelbe Fleck. Die Ausrottung von 500,000 Juden.* Paris: Editions du Carrefour, 1936, p. 5.

50. *Ibid.*, p. 5.

51. *Ibid.*, p. 267.

52. *Ibid.*, p. 5.

53. Lothar Kahn, *Insight and Action. The Life and Work of Lion Feuchtwanger.* Teaneck: Fairleigh Dickinson University, 1975, p. 18.

54. Hilde Waldo, "Lion Feuchtwanger: A Biography (July 7, 1884–December 21, 1958)" in John M. Spalek, *Lion Feuchtwanger. The Man, His Ideas, His Work.* Los Angeles: Hennessey and Ingalls, 1972, p. 12.

55. Berendsohn, p. 32.

56. For an explanation for the change of title from *Oppermann* to *Oppenheim* in the original German version, see, Kahn, p. 178. *Oppermann* remained as the title in the English translation of 1934.

57. Kahn, p. 18.

58. *Ibid.*, p. 9.

59. Lion Feuchtwanger, *Die Geschwister Oppenheim.* Amsterdam: Querido, 1934, pp. 324, 431.

60. *Ibid.*, p. 418.

61. Harold von Hofe, ed. *Lion Feuchtwanger Arnold Zweig Briefwechsel 1933–1958*. Berlin: Aufbau, 1984, pp. 113, 146, 151, 152, 158.

62. Hall, p. 8.

63. *Ibid.*, pp. 40–41.

64. A. Schnitzler, *Der Weg ins Freie*, p. 724.

65. Arthur Schnitzler, "Meine Stellung zum Zionismus." *Aufbau*, New York, May 8, 1942, pp. 17, cols. 1–3.

66. *Ibid.*, p. 17, col. 3.

67. Zweig, "Juedischer Ausdruckswille," p. 63.

LIBRARY ST. MARY'S COLLEGE

Women Writers and the Holocaust: Strategies for Survival

Ellen S. Fine

The Israeli poet Dan Pagis, who was born in 1930 in the German speaking Romanian province of Bukovina and came to Israel in 1946 after spending three years of his adolescence in a Nazi concentration camp, wrote the following poem:

Written in Pencil in the Sealed Freight Car

> Here in this carload,
> I, Eve
> with my son Abel
> If you see my older boy,
> Cain, son of Adam,
> tell him that I

In this brief but searing vision of the journey into Holocaust darkness, the death of the six million is compressed into six lines. Abel, the first victim in Biblical history, represents here all victims deported by the Nazis to a realm so unimaginable and brutal in its systematic degradation of the human species that it has been called by many survivors "another planet." Abel's older brother Cain remains outside of the doomed cattle car, for he is with the oppressors. And where is Adam, which in Hebrew means "man"? He too is absent.

What is interesting in this poetic interpretation of the post-Eden world is the central role given to Eve, mother of the two enemy brothers, and link between good and evil. Eve has given birth to Cain, the world's first assassin, who has, as Elie Wiesel points out, committed the first genocide (*Messengers of God*, 52). Eve, mother of creation, becomes a victim of her son's injustice: she is condemned to be destroyed. Yet in defiance and in desperation, she is compelled to bear witness. Her message, scrawled perhaps on a scrap of paper, and tossed through the cracks in the boxcar walls, is destined to remain unfinished, as were the life stories of millions. It is up to us, the posterity to whom the testimony is addressed, to complete the tale.

At such a critical moment, the mere attempt to write suggests a faith in the permanence of words. The literary act can be an act of resistance. The poet here clearly identifies with the woman as creator, writer, and victim, a notion essentially linked to the subject to be presently explored—women and the Holocaust. Many historians and commentators believe that the atrocities committed during the Nazi Holocaust leveled all distinctions of nationality, class, age, and gender. Yet other scholars in recent years have attempted to study the event from a particular point of view. In considering the female perspective of the Holocaust, I will first examine traumas that were unique to women; next, describe what kind of strategies for survival or coping mechanisms women adopted. I will then focus on one form of strategy, that of spiritual resistance, and in particular the use of literature to express it. While such resistance is not exclusively a female means of sustenance, it does present itself in many of the memoirs written by women.

Were there issues unique to women in the concentration camp? Scholars, such as Cynthia Haft in her book *The Theme of Nazi Concentration Camp in French Literature* (1973), and Anna Pawelcznska, a Polish survivor and author of *Values and Violence in Auschwitz: A Sociological Analysis* (1979) believe that the differentiations based on biological and social roles were eliminated in a system designed to kill all human beings and to eradicate all remnants of one's prewar existence. Others who disagree with the notion of equal treatment feel that there were differences in the camps on the basis of gender, and have begun to research the topic.

Studies on the women's experience of the Holocaust have appeared in recent years. In March 1983, more than 400 scholars, survivors, and the general public gathered in New York to attend the first conference on "Women Surviving: The Holocaust," sponsored by the Institute for Research in History and initiated by Joan Ringelheim. In 1986, Marlene Heineman published an important book entitled, *Gender and Destiny: Women Writers and the Holocaust* in which she analyzes female-centered themes and their literary expression in Holocaust memoirs and novels written by women. Another significant contribution to this topic, *Women in the Resistance and in the Holocaust* (1983), edited by Vera Laska, is a collection of eyewitness accounts of women who participated in Resistance activities throughout Europe.

In her introduction, Laska observes that women were often better suited for undercover work than men; they were quick to perceive danger, more cautious and discreet, and had more common sense. They served in various functions in the Resistance movements, such as smuggling weapons into the ghettos and even the camps, and sabotaging the manufacture of weapons in the factories. It was especially in the risky role of couriers that women proved to be courageous and resourceful. They were less suspected of illegal activities than men, and thus less easily detected.

Let us consider some of the gender distinctions between men and women that resulted in their diverse responses to extremity. In "Issues and Resources," Sybil Milton discusses certain areas where research has shown differences to be apparent. (*Proceedings of the Conference: Women Surviving*, 10–21). The first area centers around hunger and food. Women were able to tolerate hunger better than men and could endure starvation for longer periods of time than male inmates; women also had better means of sharing and extending limited supplies of food. A second area was housekeeping. Women were more occupied than men in cleaning their barracks, thus reducing the spread of diseases such as typhus. Linked to this was a concern for personal hygiene and appearance despite lack of water and sanitary facilities. Although men, too, knew that keeping clean was a form of defying the system, as Primo Levi indicates in his book, *Survival in Auschwitz,* women seemed to demonstrate more care for their appearance. It is important to point out that inmates were often selected for the gas chambers precisely on the basis of their appearance. In their memoirs, women often describe how they pinched their cheeks at the time of selection in order to look more healthy. A third area where women reacted differently from men was in bonding, and creating mutually supportive "family" networks to help one another. They developed mother substitutes. More examples of this will be discussed further on.

To add to these gender differences, Terrence Des Pres made certain observations based on testimonies written by men and women. In a letter to Joan Ringelheim, quoted in Marlene Heineman's book, *Gender and Destiny*, Des Pres said he was "struck again and again by the ways in which, under infinitely more terrible circumstances, women in places like Auschwitz and Ravensbrück made better survivors" (5). "They were more at ease in matters of intimate help. They seemed to care more for life; and being less dependent on inflated egos, as men were, where those egos were cracked and were swept away, women recovered faster and with less bitterness."

The specific female-centered issues can be divided into three main categories (Heineman, 13–37): (1) sexual abuse and humiliation, which includes rape and prostitution; (2) fear of infertility related to the stoppage of menstruation; and (3) maternity and childbirth. The sexual assault, both verbal and physical, occurred at the initial stage of the camp experience and is described in almost all memoirs by women. Women were forced to parade naked in front of SS guards. Stripped bare of their clothes, their hair, their name, they were subject to the verbal abuse, stares, and prodding fingers of their oppressors, and felt extremely vulnerable, powerless, humiliated. Rape seems to have affected a minority of women inmates, and prostitution existed in varying degrees in the brothels set up by the SS in certain camps. As for menstruation, many accounts refer to the awkwardness or danger of menstruation when it occurred, and how it warranted a beating from block leaders. Almost all women eventually stopped menstruating because of the harsh conditions and poor food of the camp. They were forced to live with the fear of losing their identity as women, of becoming permanently infertile.

Maternity and childbirth figure most prominently in Holocaust literature written by women. The theme of the mother-child relationship with its many variations recurs often, and is depicted in heartrending episodes. Upon arrival at the camps, selection took place on the basis of age, health, and gender. Adolescents watched their mothers silently march toward the death factories, and mothers saw their children being taken away. Women with small children especially were targeted for immediate extermination. Therefore, being a mother directly affected the chances for survival; being a father did not. On occasion, able-bodied mothers fit for labor suddenly realized as they paraded before Mengele and the other SS doctors that they were being selected just because they had young children. Most often, they clung to their children and marched straight to their death, but in a few instances, they walked ahead of them, deafening themselves to the penetrating cries of "Mama, Mama!" The will to live was at odds with the maternal instinct. This is an example of what Lawrence Langer in his book, *Versions of Survival: The Holocaust and the Human Spirit*, calls "a choiceless choice," opting between two unacceptable evils (72). It is an example of a negative strategy for survival, a means of staying alive, of cheating death, but one which brings about great moral agony.

In her memoir, *Five Chimneys*, Olga Lengyel, the wife of a well-known doctor from Kolozsvár (Cluj), Hungary, confesses to an unforgiveable choice that was to burden her with guilt for the rest of her life. At the moment of selection in Auschwitz, she and her mother were waved by the SS to the adult group which meant life. Her younger son was classed with the children and the aged. The selector hesitated in front of her older son who was big for his age, saying that he must be more than twelve years old. "No," Olga protested, thinking that he would be protected from arduous labor if he did not go with the adults. She then persuaded her mother to follow the children to take care of them. "The world understands that I could not have known, but in my heart the terrible feeling persists that I could have, I might have saved them," Lengyel reveals (13). The concentration camp universe transformed the victim into an oppressor.

Olga Lengyel's feeling of responsibility for the death of her children is carried a step further in her role as physician in the camp infirmary. When a baby was delivered in the camps, mother and child were condemned to die. As another Hungarian inmate-physician, Dr. Gisella Perl has confirmed: "The greatest crime in Auschwitz was to be pregnant." Only when the infant did not survive was the mother spared. Mrs. Lengyel and her four colleagues on the hospital staff were faced with a monstrous dilemma. After much reflection, they finally decided that they had to save the mothers. The birth took place in secrecy. The doctor pinched the infant's nostrils, and when it opened its mouth to breathe it was given a dose of a lethal product. In other instances, it was given an injection (Nomberg-Przytyk, 69), or the pregnancy was interrupted, causing a premature delivery (Perl). In that way, the dead child passed for stillborn. Lengyel comments:

> And so, the Germans succeeded in making murderers of even us. To this day the picture of those murdered babies haunts me. . . . Who knows? Perhaps we killed a Pasteur, a Mozart, an Einstein. Even had those infants been destined to uneventful lives, our crimes were no less terrible. The only meager consolation is that by these murders we saved the mothers. Without our intervention they would have endured worse sufferings, for they would have been thrown into the crematory oven while still alive (111).

And Perl reveals: "No one will ever know what it meant to me to destroy those babies, but if I had not done it, both mother and child would have been cruelly murdered." Surely then, this is an act of resistance, a strategy for survival, but at what cost? The healer becomes a killer in the unreal reality that was Auschwitz.

If the inhabitants of this desolate universe were forced to devise ways of keeping alive that often went against life itself, they also managed to find positive means of sustaining the body and the spirit. Traces of solidarity persist despite the Nazi attempt to destroy all human bonds. In her memoir, *Fragments of Isabella,* Isabella Leitner tells of losing her mother and youngest sister at the moment of selection. Yet, she and her other three sisters managed to stay together until just before liberation. She speaks of the terror of separation and the awesome burden each sister had of staying alive because of the others. Her sister, Rachel, confessed: "Alone, I won't make it. I don't want to make it. Whatever effort I am making now is all for you. I no longer care to live—unless, and only if, we are together" (36). Gizelle Hersh, too, watched over her three younger sisters, as her mother's final words were engraved in her memory, "Gizelle, Save the Children!" which became the title of her book. She internalized her mother, and took her place as head of the family.

Anguished by the loss of their mothers, their children, and their siblings, some of the women formed substitute families and support systems. Within those systems, they created mother surrogates. Charlotte Delbo, a member of the French Resistance movement, gives examples of collective caring in her poetic testimony, *Aucun de nous ne reviendra* (1965) (English translation: *None of Us Will Return* [1968]). Delbo wrote down her impressions immediately after coming back from the camps, but kept them in a drawer for 20 years before she was ready to publish them. In her account, Delbo describes the daily roll call: the inmates had to line up at 4 A.M. and stand motionless for hours in the icy wind, dressed only in a light garment. They invented a way to make the cold more bearable:

> With her neck retracted into her shoulders, her chest pulled in, each woman puts her hands under the arms of the women in front of her. In the first row, they cannot do this, and they are rotated. Chest to back, we stand huddled together, and although we thus set up a common circulation for all, a common circulatory system, we are all frozen (71–72).

Despite the attempt to resist the subhuman conditions by bonding together, on one occasion, Charlotte succumbs to the cold, loses consciousness, and slips silently into the snow. She comes to, jolted by the slap that her friend, Viva, is giving her across her cheeks, as her name is being called again and again. "It is the voice of my mother that I hear," Delbo says.

> The voice grows hard: "Heads up. On your feet." And I feel that I cling to Viva as much as a child clings to its mother. I cling to the woman who has kept me from falling into the slush, into the snow from which one does not get up again. And I must struggle to make

a choice between the consciousness that is suffering and this surrender that was bliss, and I choose because Viva says to me: "Heads up. On your feet." . . . I regain possession of myself. . . . I am in the midst of my comrades. I take my place once more in the poor communal warmth that our contact creates (73–74).

The mother surrogate is a source of sustenance, endowing the victim with strength to continue the struggle, and demonstrating that vestiges of humanity remain in a world destined to systematically demolish human dignity and the sense of self.

Another moving example of a mother surrogate is evoked by Delbo in *None of Us Will Return*. Charlotte is digging at the bottom of a ditch with two of her companions, Lulu and Viva. They talk about plans for the return; sharing this hope makes it possible. A female SS guard comes along and forces Charlotte's friends to leave the ditch. The SS know the fear that every woman has of being separated from the others, of being alone, Delbo observes. Terrified, overcome with despair, Charlotte wants to lie down in the mud at the bottom of the ditch and die. Finally, she is told to climb out and join her friends on their work detail. "I can't take it any more," she tells Lulu (117). "Get behind me so they don't see you. You can have a good cry," Lulu says gently. Charlotte does not want to cry, but the tears spill down her cheeks endlessly. Lulu works, keeps watch, and turns around occasionally to wipe her friend's face with her sleeve. Eventually she says, "That's all now. Come work." And Charlotte, touched by the nurturing offered to her in the most miserable of circumstances, comments: "With so much kindness I am not ashamed of having cried. It is as though I had cried on my mother's breast" (118). Thus, the bonds of friendship helped women to replace their lost mothers and children with newly formed family networks, a means of defying the dehumanization of *l'univers concentrationnaire*.

Nurturing not only occurred through a communal sharing of emotional pain. In several accounts by woman survivors, exchanges of another kind constituted a form of resistance: the sharing of memory.

Hunger was the principal obsession of all camp inmates. To combat the slow death by starvation, women traded recipes. Livia Bitton Jackson, who was deported to Auschwitz from Hungary at the age of 13 and managed to stay with her mother throughout the transfers from one camp to another, describes in her memoir, *Elli: Coming of Age in the Holocaust* (1980), how women working 12 hours a day leveling a hilltop for construction talked mostly about the food they cooked at home "in prehistoric times," as she says. They compose dishes "like shipwrecked musicians thinking musical notes out loud"

(94). The women also talk about their former lives, their youth, their first loves, their families. Remembering is painful at first, but the starved prisoners are nourished by their past. "The shared pain forges a strong bond," Jackson notes (94).

A survivor in Charlotte Delbo's account *Mesure de nos jours* also stresses the importance of sharing personal memories and stories. The past becomes a form of protection from the horror, a means of keeping the self intact: "Each one of us related our life thousands of times over, resurrecting our childhood, the times of freedom and happiness, in order to assure ourselves that we had lived it. . . . Our past was for us a safeguard and a comfort" (50).

Of all the strategies for survival and for preserving memory, the one that attests most to the triumph of the human spirit is the recollection of literature. Remembering, reciting, and sometimes even composing fragments of literary works served as forms of spiritual nourishment. Literature became "equipment for living," as Kenneth Burke puts it in another context in *The Philosophy of Literary Form* (51;262). Reaching out to literature in the midst of the Holocaust despair served different functions: it was a way of holding on to one's heritage and tradition; of affirming one's identity as a human being in the face of brutality and degradation; it was a vehicle of communion and sharing. Literature became an instrument of transcendence, a means of partaking in a realm larger than oneself. In the ghettos and camps both men and women responded to catastrophe by turning to reading, writing, and reciting literature. This has been well documented in such studies as David Roskies' exemplary volume, *Against the Apocalypse: Responses to Catastrophe in Modern Jewish Culture* (1984), and Michel Borwicz's *Ecrits des condamnés à mort sous l'occupation nazie* (1973).

Key questions that must be addressed are: Is there a connection between literature and the struggle to survive? How can literature be considered a mode of resistance? In the camps, actions of organized revolt and resistance were undertaken in opposition to the Nazis: for example, smuggling food, shoes, and clothing out of the warehouses into the rest of the camp; sabotage in the weapons factory; substituting names of those who had died for those selected for the gas chambers; smuggling arms from outside of the camps with the help of partisan groups and the political underground; and even blowing up the crematorium in Auschwitz. But in addition to these dramatic acts of defiance, there was the more covert and inward resistance where one fought to keep intact one's dignity, one's identity, one's humanity. This was spiritual resistance.

We have observed instances in which prisoners physically and emotionally supported one another in the most extreme of circumstances. According to Frieda Aaron, a survivor of the Warsaw Ghetto uprising, and of various camps including Maidanek, as well as being a poet and a scholar, a link also exists between helping one another and participating in literary activity. In a recent article on "Yiddish and Polish Poetry in the Ghettos and Camps" published in *Modern Language Studies*, Aaron notes.

> In the camps where writing materials were not available, neophyte poets occasionally emerged and could be seen huddled together on bunk beds, composing song and poems and sometimes committing them to memory. . . . The initial purpose of this creativity was neither the poem for itself nor even the poem as bearer of witness—since without writing materials this was hardly possible—but rather the *process*. For it was the process that helped to keep the soul alive. . . . What is most significant, is that *these moments of creativity were the ones when the spirit to help each other was most apparent.* . . . Creativity helped to mobilize coping mechanisms of which mutual help was an important part (72). (my emphasis)

Literature, then, on some level in the Holocaust kingdom, became a means of mobilizing support systems and was part of a joint effort to stay alive. The prevailing form of literary expression in the camps was poetry, for it nourished one's emotions and was more readily accessible than the other genres. The "process" manifests itself in the reciting and writing of poetry, and can be found throughout texts written by women. The reciting of poetry, for example, often took place in the camp infirmary. Polish survivor, Sara Nomberg-Przytyk, in her vivid narration of life in a death camp, *Auschwitz: True Tales from a Grotesque Land*, describes a cultural evening that took place in the women's infirmary (114–117). French women sang French songs about Paris; some Czechs sang about "those who 'defy the wind'"; she herself sang a Russian song about the red sky. The conductor of the camp orchestra played Hungarian and gypsy melodies on the violin, and somebody recited a poem. Nomberg-Przytyk reflects that, in the beginning, these "friendly get-togethers" struck her as indecent. The contrast between death's presence hovering over them, and the poems, stories, songs and even jokes, was unbearable. After eight months in Auschwitz, however, she too sang and laughed at these get-togethers, even though she had daily to step over corpses lying in her path: "I had imbibed all of the terrors of Auschwitz and lived," she says (115). Yet, she confesses to being unsure as to whether this ability to adapt was good or bad.

A member of the French Resistance, teacher and poet Micheline Maurel, in *Un camp très ordinaire* relates how she and a crippled inmate, Irenka, spoke of literature and grammar, and recited French and Polish poems to each other in the infirmary of the women's camp, Neubrandebourg, a branch of Ravensbrück. Suffering from a high fever caused by scabies that were infected, Maurel nonetheless wrote poetry on scraps of paper that the *blokowa*, or head of the infirmary barracks, procured for her. She would read her verse to Irenka, the *blokowa*, and even the doctor, as she evoked images that celebrated the natural beauty and fertility of her native Provence, sharply contrasting with the barren and sinister winter landscape of Germany:

> Vingt-cinq janvier! chez nous les amandiers
> fleurissent,
> L'herbe pousse plus verte au pied des oliviers. . .
>
> [January twenty-five! at home the almond trees
> flower/ The grass grows greener at the foot of
> the olive trees. . .] (78)

When Irenka was "selected," along with a group of Russian patients stricken with tuberculosis, to be loaded onto trucks and be taken to a "rest camp," Micheline suffered enormously from the loss of her spiritual and intellectual companion. She was moved to another room in the infirmary. Her new neighbor was French, and a professor of philosophy. Lying on her bunk bed, sick with dysentery, the professor recited by heart the verse of Mallarmé, Valéry, and Baudelaire to Micheline (80–81).

Later on, when she returned to her barracks, Maurel and her bunkmates continued to quote the poetry of Ronsard, Lamartine, Victor Hugo, Musset, and Baudelaire. Reconstituting each line from memory was a collective effort, and encouraged bonding among the women, even among those who were not acquainted with the great French writers and were listening to them for the first time. In their longing for the lyrical, the women preferred poems with themes not related to misery, prison, or death. Maurel observes that Baudelaire's sonnets were especially popular because they were easier to remember. Poems such as "La Vie antérieure," "Correspondances," and "Re-cueillement" were often repeated. However, it is interesting that there were some lines in "Recueillement" ["Meditation"] that none of them could recall. When Maurel read the poem after liberation from the camps, she understood why. "Recueillement" begins:

> Sois sage, ô ma Douleur, et tiens-toi plus tranquille.
> Tu réclamais le Soir; il descend; le voici:
> Une atmosphère obscure enveloppe la ville,
> Aux uns portant la paix, aux autres le souci.

> [Be tranquil, O my Sorrow, and be wise.
> The Evening comes, is here, for which you sought:
> The Dusk, wrapping the city in disguise,
> Care unto some, to others peace has brought.]
>
> trans. Barbara Gibbs.

The unremembered lines that follow are:

> Pendant que des mortels la multitude vile,
> Sous le fouet du Plaisir, ce bourreau sans merci,
> Va cueillir des remords dans la fête servile. . .

> [Now while the sordid multitude with shame
> Obeying Pleasure's whip and merciless sway,
> Go gathering remorse in servile game. . .]

Baudelaire is lamenting here the condition of the "sordid multitude," that is to say, the decadent bourgeois city dwellers who shamefully succumb to vice and are oppressed by too much pleasure, "ce bourreau sans merci," a situation that seemed most enviable to the women prisoners whose own oppression differed radically, and who could not identify with Baudelaire's condemnation of the capitalist society, comments Maurel (111–112).

Micheline Maurel came to be known as the camp poet and her notebooks of poetry were secretly circulated among the inmates. Sometimes she would compose poems upon request, to be offered as a gift to another prisoner, or as a form of catharsis. For example, a young French woman asked Maurel to write a poem about her love for the two young children she had left at home in France. The poem made the woman cry, but also gave her solace and something to cling to (113). In conditions of extremity, poetry thus became, as Ilona Karmel, author of the novel, *An Estate of Memory*, has stated in an interview: "a kind of pipeline to psychological, spiritual survival" (Pomerantz, 81).

In his book, *Ecrits des condamnés à mort sous l'occupation nazie (1939–45)*, Michel Borwicz cites another instance in which a poem was presented as a gift to soothe suffering and save the soul. Maria Zarebinska, in "A propos des poèmes de Krystyna Zywuslka" describes a poignant incident that took place in Birkenau. This is how she relates it: A woman prisoner in fairly good health sneaks into the women's infirmary. She slips to the back and says softly to a group of women that she knows personally: "I bring you a present: a poem written by one of our comrades." She lifts her head, stands on her toes in order to be heard by the sick women lying on the highest bunks, and recites the poem. One woman weeps, one clenches her fists passionately, and we all beg her to give us the text. Someone has a piece of paper, another a pencil, and within 10 minutes, the poem is copied. The despair of the empty hours spent lying in bed will be filled: . . . we will learn the poem by heart. Since then, I always heard the poems of Christine. . . . we recited them everywhere, while we dug ditches, coming back from the fields, and on the bunks at night (Borwicz, 84–85).

To sustain her spirit, Charlotte Delbo also recited poetry or recounted plays and novels to her comrades as they dug in the marshes and waded in the mud. "It was to stay alive, to keep my memory intact, to be in touch with myself, to be reassured," she affirms in La mémoire et les jours (12). Yet, Delbo feels a need to clarify her belief that literature was not a form of escape. Even if her love for, and deep knowledge of, literature helped her in the daily battle to survive, it did not allow her to forget that only a short distance away the crematoria continued to burn human flesh. "This [reciting poetry] never for a moment obliterated what I was living through. Remembering was a victory over the horror, but it did not diminish anything. Reality was always present," she notes (12).

Of the many woman writers who described their experience in the death camps, Delbo is one of the most astute and articulate with regard to the role of memory and literature in l'univers concentrationnaire. Born in 1913, she was a student of philosophy before she began to work full time as assistant to the well-known theater director Louis Jouvet, and thus was immersed in literature before the war. In 1941, she was safe in Buenos Aires, working with Jouvet who was on tour. After reading about a friend who was executed because of her work in the Resistance, Delbo chose to return to France. She joined her politically active husband, George Dudach, and worked for the French Resistance. They were arrested by the Nazis in March 1942, and a few months later, in May 1942, her husband was executed. Delbo was imprisoned in France until January 24, 1943, when she was deported to Birkenau with a convoy of 230 French women political prisoners, who had taken an active part in the Resistance. The voyage, and members of the group, are portrayed in Delbo's book, *Le convoi du 24 janvier* (1965). Of 230 women who left, only 49 returned.

Charlotte Delbo also wrote other books about her experience in the concentration camps: a trilogy entitled *Auschwitz et Apres* consisting of *Aucun de nous ne reviendra* (1965); *Une connaissance inutile* (1970), and *Mesure de nos Jours (1971)*. She published a play, *Qui rapportera ces paroles?* (1974), translated into English as *Who Will Carry the Word?* as well as a long essay called *Spectres, mes compagnons* (1977) that was translated into English in *The Massachusetts Review*. Her last book, *La mémoire et les jours*, a series of incidents, images, poems, and reflections on the past and the present, all related to the agony of Auschwitz, was published in 1985, shortly after her death.

Before Charlotte was deported to Auschwitz, she spent over a year in prison, much of it in solitary confinement. In her piece, "Phantoms, My Companions," written in the form of a letter addressed to Louis Jouvet, she describes her time in prison: "You are alone in a dark hovel where muffled sounds set you wondering whether you dream. Nothing sees you or visits you, you are abandoned, forgotten. . . . A region of the imagination dries up, a source of poetry" (19). Despite the total seclusion and the fear of losing her belief in the magical world of the imagination, Charlotte manages to people her cell with characters from novels and plays. First, Fabrice del Dongo, the protagonist of Stendhal's *La Chartreuse de Parme* visits her:

> Fabrice's presence was more than mere presence. The life of a literary character is more intense than that of a human being. . . . In prison, a literary character is filled with a particular vivacity. He flourishes with greater freedom. Perhaps it is only there that he can be truly himself. He is alone, and heeded; he finds in his companion undisputed attentiveness and interest. (16)

Giraudoux's Ondine also enters Delbo's cell and stays with her when it is time for her final goodbye to her husband before he is shot by the Gestapo.

When Charlotte finally leaves the citadel for her journey to the East, her literary companions abandon her. For two days and two nights in the dark cattle car, there is silence until finally she hears a voice from among the shadows. She is happy to recognize that it is the voice of Alceste. The character of *The Misanthrope* has set forth with her to the barren land where she is headed. Charlotte converses with Alceste and realizes she is tutoying him, speaking in an intimate way to a close friend. "Is it in order to leave for the desert that you are going with me? A curious definition of the word," she says to

him. Alceste replies: "True deserts hardly exist in our world, except
in that remote part of the planet where you are going." ("Phantoms,
My Companions," 23); "It is the true desert, where all human passions
are abolished. Here, man divests himself of the human. Here man
stops being man, stops being" (27). And Charlotte understands that
Alceste, the hero of a play, was also capable of human heroism, that
he was accompanying her by choice where she was forced to go, that
he alone, with his thirst for the absolute, had the courage to follow
her. And yet, as the freight cars reach Auschwitz and the shrieking
commands of SS guards and barks of howling dogs greet the numbed
passengers, Alceste, wrapped in his black cape, jumps out of the
wagon and disappears into the night. He is unable to cross the
threshold into the realm of this totally inhuman landscape.

"I never found him again throughout this sojourn in hell," Delbo
states. "I knew that Alceste had left, never to return. . . . Where
human beings suffered and died, dramatic characters could not live
. . . dramatic characters could only live in the society of men" (29).

While Delbo's reflection about losing the ability to summon the
imagination during times of extreme duress is comprehensible, it is
curious that in this essay, "Phantoms, My Companions," published
first in the English translation in 1971, and then in French in 1977,
she acknowledges the loss of Alceste during her camp stay. One
wonders if she has chosen intentionally to state that a literary presence
could no longer offer solace in extremity, or if she, in fact, forgot
that Alceste did indeed reenter the stage, for she devoted a short
section of her book, *Une connaissance inutile*, published earlier in
1970, to *Le Misanthrope* (122–125). Delbo relates how in Ravensbrück
she met a gypsy woman selling all kinds of objects, among which
was the Petits Classiques Larousse edition of *Le Misanthrope*. Without
hesitation, Charlotte exchanged her ration of bread for Molière's play.
Her bunkmates understood the nature of this choice, and when she
returned to the barracks, clutching the precious volume, each friend
cut a piece from her own crust of bread to compensate Charlotte.
Every night, Delbo learned a fragment of the play by heart, and
repeated it in the early morning hours during roll call until she knew
the whole play. Delbo hid the book under her dress, next to her heart
for the rest of her stay in the camp.

The last night in Ravensbrück, on the eve of liberation, after Delbo
had enjoyed her first cup of coffee in 27 months, she felt a bizarre
kind of rush. Stricken with anxiety, she felt she was going to die of
suffocation. As she gasped for air and unbuttoned her dress, she
threw *Le Misanthrope* to the ground, for it was obstructing her breathing.
The next night, as she was undressing, a free woman in Denmark,

she noticed that she had forgotten to bring her *Misanthrope* (*Connaissance*, 168–173). Thus, does Alceste leave her at the most critical moments, both upon entering and leaving *l'univers concentrationnaire*.

The act of forgetting to bring the play with her is charged with significance. Delbo had already committed it to memory, and no longer needed the actual text. But more important, she no longer had to seek refuge in a stronghold of the past as a means of keeping herself and her memory alive. The return to Paris revealed further ironies with regard to literature and memory. A gulf existed between herself and others. She felt absent, in a void: "I was floating in a present without reality" (*Mesure de nos jours*, 14). Friends came to her room, bringing flowers and books, but the unopened books piled up on her night table, "within reach, out of my reach," as she puts it (*Mesure*, 14). They were useless objects that had nothing to do with life; she thought everything inside of them was false, empty. Auschwitz had killed her faith in the imaginary, illusionary universe created by a literary work. The faculty of memory that had empowered her to survive the death encounter was now working against her. Memory of the atrocities had deadened her ability both to live life in the present, and to read books.

However, one morning she was awakened by a strangely familiar voice that rose from the long-forgotten past. She did not know whose voice it was knocking at the door of her memory, but was convinced that she would soon recognize it. Finally: "Alceste! Alceste! C'est toi?"

"You're still there? Do you remember me?"

"I always remembered you. It was you who had forgotten me. Why did you wish to forget me?" Alceste answered.

"Forgive me," Charlotte told him. "I never wanted to forget you. Why did you wait so long to come back to me?"

And Alceste replied: "I never left you. . . . I was in the kingdom of the shadows all the time that you were there yourself. I've returned only because you've returned" (*Spectres*, 35).

What joy Charlotte experiences to see Alceste once again. "Everything was coming back," she says, "words and the ability to speak them, gestures and the strength to make them" ("Phantoms, My Faithful Ones," 314–15). Alceste sits by her and hands her one book, thereby handing her back all books. Charlotte understands that Alceste has led her back to herself and that she has returned—or at least a part of her has returned.

Just as literature in the dominion of death was a life-sustaining force, a means of bonding and support, of moral and spiritual sustenance, so too for Charlotte Delbo and many other survivors after the Holocaust, the ability to rediscover literature, to read, and especially to *write* their personal testimonies—*to bear witness* for those many Eves in the cattle cars whose life stories were to remain unfinished—this mission of memory has become the survivors' principal strategy of survival and ultimately, the justification for their existence.

WORKS CITED

Frieda Aaron, "Yiddish and Polish Poetry in the Ghettos and Camps." *Modern Language Studies*, vol. 19, no. 1, 1989, pp. 72–87.

Charles Baudelaire, *Flowers of Evil.* Eds. and trans. Marthiel and Jackson Mathews. New York: New Directions, 1955.

Michel Borwicz, *Ecrits des condamnés à mort sous l'occupation nazie (1939–45).* Paris: Idées/Gallimard, 1973.

Kenneth Burke, *The Philosophy of Literary Form.* New York: Vintage, 1941.

Charlotte Delbo, *Une connaissance inutile.* Paris: Editions de Minuit, 1970.

_____ *Le Convoi du 24 janvier.* Paris: Minuit, 1965.

_____ *La mémoire et les jours.* Paris: Berg international, 1985.

_____ *Mesure de nos jours.* Paris: Minuit, 1971.

_____ *None of Us Will Return.* (English trans., by John Githens. Boston: Beacon Press, 1968 of *Aucun de nous ne reviendra*, 1965.

_____ "Phantoms, My Companions." Trans. Rosette Lamont. *Massachusetts Review*, vol. 12, 1971, pp. 10–30.

_____ "Phantoms, My Faithful Ones." Trans. Rosette Lamont. *Massachusetts Review*, vol. 14, 1973, pp. 310–315.

_____ *Spectres, mes compagnons.* Lausanne: Maurice Bridel, 1977.

Cynthia Haft, *The Theme of Nazi Concentration Camp in French Literature.* The Hague: Mouton, 1973.

Marlene Heineman, *Gender and Destiny: Women Writers and the Holocaust.* Westport: Greenwood Press, 1986.

Gizelle Hersh, and Peggy Mann. *"Gizelle, Save the Children!"* New York: Everest House, 1980.

Livia Bitton Jackson, *Elli: Coming of Age in the Holocaust.* New York: Times Books, 1980.

Esther Katz, and Joan Ringelheim, *eds. Proceedings of the Conference, Women Surviving the Holocaust.* New York: The Institute for Research in History, 1983.

Lawrence Langer, *Versions of Survival: The Holocaust and the Human Spirit.* Albany: State University of New York Press, 1982.

Vera Laska, *ed. Women in the Resistance and in the Holocaust: The Voices of Eyewitnesses.* Westport: Greenwood Press, 1983.

Isabella Leitner, *Fragments of Isabella: A Memoir of Auschwitz.* New York: Thomas Cromwell, 1978.

Olga Lengyel, *Five Chimneys: The Story of Auschwitz.* Trans. Paul B. Weiss. Chicago: Ziff-Davis, 1947.

Primo Levi, *Survival in Auschwitz.* Trans. Stuart Woolf. New York: Collier Books, 1969.

Micheline Maurel, *Un camp très ordinaire.* Paris: Editions de Minuit, 1957. *An Ordinary Camp.* Trans. Margaret S. Summers. New York: Simon and Schuster, 1958. (References are to the French edition with my translations.)

Sara Nomberg-Przytyk, *Auschwitz: True Tales from a Grotesque Land.* Trans. Roslyn Hirsch. Edited by Eli Pfefferkorn and David H. Hirsch. Chapel Hill: University of North Carolina Press, 1985.

Dan Pagis, "Written in Pencil in the Sealed Freight Car." *The Penguin Book of Hebrew Verse.* Ed. T. Carmi. New York: Viking Press, 1981.

Anna Pawelczynska, *Values and Violence in Auschwitz: A Sociological Analysis.* Berkeley: University of California Press, 1979.

Gisella Perl, "Out of Death, A Zest for Life." *New York Times,* November 15, 1982.

Gayle Pomerantz, "An Exploration of the Literature by Women Survivors of the Holocaust." Senior Thesis. Brandeis University, 1983.

David G. Roskies, *Against the Apocalypse: Responses to Catastrophe in Modern Jewish Culture.* Cambridge: Harvard University Press, 1984.

Elie Wiesel, *Messengers of God: Biblical Portraits and Legends.* New York: Pocket Book Editions, 1977.

Maria Zarebinska, "A propos des poèmes de Krystyna Zywuslka" in *Oswiecim.* Warsaw: Ksiazka, 1946, pp. 265–267.

---

*All translations from the French editions are mine unless otherwise noted.

Ashes and Hope:
The Holocaust in Second
Generation American Literature

Alan L. Berger

Seeking to forge a new link in the chain of Jewish memory, Elie Wiesel compares the experience of Abraham and Isaac to the experiences of survivors and their children. "The *Akedah*, after all," observes Wiesel, "was not consummated. The testimony of our life and death will not vanish. Our memories will not die with us."[1] Wiesel's observation underscores both the existence of a second generation literature of the Holocaust and the solemn task he ascribes to such writings. It also raises a host of questions about the relationship of this literature to the *Shoah*. How, for example, does the second generation "remember" an event that occurred before its birth, and yet is the most important event in its life? What are the distinctive icons and images of the Holocaust employed in second generation writings? What is the relationshp of this literature to other Jewish-American writing? What is the likely role that second generation literature will play as the Holocaust's literary future in American novels assumes increased importance? While all of these issues constitute legitimate inquiry, it is not possible to address each one in this paper. Rather, my focus is on the post-Auschwitz meaning of covenant and Jewish identity as these concerns are addressed in selected examples of second generation literature.

PROBLEMATICS

Collectively, second generation literature constitutes what Alvin Rosenfeld terms a special dimension of Holocaust literature—"the type that is written by . . . the kinds of survivors, those who were never there but know more than the outlines of the place."[2] Theologically, second generation covenant grappling occurs against the background of their parents' Holocaust experience, which underscored the ambiguity of the divine-human relationship. The children's search for post-Auschwitz Jewish affirmation is conducted despite the knowledge that, in Irving Greenberg's words, "destruction can take place, that the sea will not be split for them, that the divine has self-limited, and they have additional responsibilities."[3] The covenantal quest of this generation instances what Greenberg terms the "voluntary covenant," one which stresses the obligation of the human covenantal partner. Consequently, decoding this literature serves to reveal much about the literary, psychosocial, and theological dimensions of post-Auschwitz Judaism in America. But how does this generation write about the *Shoah?* What are its distinctive images of the horror?

The issue is well framed by Norma Rosen's contention that Holocaust imagery bears a "second life."[4] Tales and stories from the *Shoah* therefore involve a double rite of passage which moves from the particular to the universal and then back to the particular. Literature exemplifying this second life includes Wiesel's *Night,* Susan Fromberg Schaeffer's *Anya,* and Cynthia Ozick's "The Shawl." Rosen correctly observes that *Night* has been read by fathers and sons all over the world. Consequently, she conjectures that in the pages of this stark and powerful memoir "whole generations of fathers and sons see the mirroring of themselves."[5] Similarly, young nursing mothers, in the safety of their American homes, will experience the pain of mothers who, in the kingdom of night, had to watch their own children suffer and perish. Rosen's argument is both persuasive and troubling. She rightly emphasizes the necessity of reading tales of the Holocaust. These stories transform their sensitive readers and make them into types of witnesses.[6]

Yet Rosen's position, implicitly, lulls the reader into thinking that Holocaust literature consists of only two models: the first is that written by the witnesses themselves. The second is that composed by those who, as she termed them in an earlier essay, are "witnesses through the imagination."[7] Clearly, there is no quarrel with the first type of writing. The testimony of witnesses has, in fact, been compared to a new sacred text.[8] The second model, however, has resulted in a great variety of writing. Some of it has been quite sensitive, such as Saul Bellow's *Mr. Sammler's Planet,* and Rosen's own *Touching Evil.* There also, however, have been gross distortions and misuse of the Holocaust in literature written by nonwitnessing authors. In America one thinks immediately of Philip Roth's *The Ghostwriter* and William Styron's *Sophie's Choice,* both of which, whatever their authors' intentions, have served primarily to divert attention from the *Shoah* as an epoch-making event, focusing instead on various personal motives. The Holocaust has, in any case, entered the public domain and is thereby subject to all manner of whim and caprice.

But there exists a third type of writing about the *Shoah* which is written neither by witnesses nor by "witnesses through the imagination." Children of Holocaust survivors occupy, in fact, a distinctive position in writing about the impact of their parents' Holocaust experiences on their own lives. The relationship of these post-Auschwitz American Jews to the catastrophe of European Judaism is intensely personal. They constitute a generation that is both first and last; defined in the words of Menachem Rosensaft, one of their number, as "the first to be born after the Holocaust and the last to have a direct link with that Eastern European Jewish existence that was so brutally annihilated."[9] The Holocaust reflections of this generation are, therefore, more than of literary interest; they serve as a powerful theological statement.

Within second generation writing there appears to exist two orientations. One is a specifically Judaic quest consisting of an attempt to wrestle with covenantal Judaism and personal identity after Auschwitz. The other type, while not at all ignoring the first quest, emphasizes what it perceives to be the *Shoah's* universal message, which is interpreted as an imperative to improve society at large. These orientations conform broadly to the suggestions made in earlier studies. Jack Nusan Porter, for example, rightly argues that while it is too early to contend that there exists a "second generation syndrome," in terms of the kinds of psychic problems exhibited by some members of the witnessing generation, a type of "sociopolitical syndrome" may in fact exist. He observes that "many children of survivors are committed to making sense out of the Holocaust and this can lead to a wide variety of creative political and religious action."[10] Such action may be either particularist, or universalist. Bela Savran and Eva Fogelman, writing specifically of psychological issues concerning grown children of survivors, speak in terms of mission rather than syndrome. Their study notes that such children see themselves as a direct link to the obliterated past.[11] Consequently, many children of survivors feel that they have a "mission to witness to an event and a culture they never really knew."[12]

Both of these psychosocial studies were concluded before the emergence of a substantial number of second generation novels. However, it is now possible to test the accuracy of these conclusions. Among second generation writings the clearest examples of a particularist response are seen in Barbara Finkelstein's *Summer Long-a-Coming* (1987), Thomas Friedmann's *Damaged Goods* (1984), and Art

Spiegelman's *Maus* (1986); the universalist orientation is best seen in Carol Ascher's *The Flood* (1987) and Julie Salamon's *White Lies* (1987).

PARTICULARISTIC

Barbara Finkelstein, a free-lance writer, is a daughter of Holocaust survivors, both of whom are pious Jews. She articulates in a lecture the difference between survivors and their children, claiming that the *"Shoah* is not my center, it's my shadow, like footsteps walking up behind me."[13] Yet, in the same lecture she also notes the *Shoah's* continuing impact, claiming that the "Holocaust casts a shadow too wide for me to escape."[14] Her novel, *Summer Long-a-Coming,*[15] set amidst the turmoil of the sixties, concerns the problems of Jewish identity which beset an adolescent daughter of Holocaust survivors. Rukhl and Yankl Szuster are orthodox Jews who, after the war, become poultry farmers in southern New Jersey. They speak Yiddish, distrust the outside world, and discuss the Holocaust with their survivor friends and relatives, but not their own children. Their oldest is a son, Sheiye, who is both symbolically related to the Messiah, and inescapably attracted to evil. Their two daughters, Brantzche and Perel, are inseparable and both are in constant conflict with their brother. The novel combines psychological and theological components of post-Auschwitz identity as the fifteen-year-old Brantzche narrates the story of Sheiye's accidental killing of their nine-year-old sister.

The novel's two books contain 26 chapters, of which 6 are in the form of historical depositions given by Rukhl and Yankl to a Yad Vashem historian. Finkelstein's use of Israel's national archive, monument, and museum to the victims and martyrs of the Holocaust, both anchors the novel and emphasizes the necessity of hearing survivors' tales. Finkelstein neither invents her own stories nor does she put the second generation on a par with their survivor parents. Rather, she portrays children of survivors as being different not only from their parents but from their American peers as well. Brantzche, for example, describes her relationship to her mother in a characteristically revealing fashion: "I felt as I always did with Mama in public," observes Brantzche, "She and I were in on a secret, but I didn't know what it was" (230). *Summer Long-a-Coming* tells the tale of Brantzche's attempt to discover the contents of this secret.

Brantzche's identity as a member of the second generation reveals the complexities of the survivor parent-child relationship. Like Spiegelman's *Maus* and Friedmann's *Damaged Goods,* Finkelstein's novel presents the reader with a look at how the Holocaust's legacy can be communicated both verbally and nonverbally. The burden of the

Holocaust, in fact, appears at times to overwhelm the fifteen-year-old girl. Brantzche is not only "scared" of her mother, but also confides that often before falling asleep she has a fantasy in which she rolls her mother into a tiny ball and throws her across time and space into 1942 Poland. Brantzche knows only that her parents' continued suffering is too much for her to bear. She understands neither why her parents spend hours arguing over the chronology of the war, nor why "history wasn't finished abusing" the Szuster family.

The parents, for their part, cling to traditional ways, teaching the daughters to *daven* (pray) and to obey scrupulously the laws of *Shabbat* (Sabbath). Rukhl and Yankl continue to commemorate their Holocaust dead by lighting *yahrzeit* (memorial) candles. These candles are, in fact, one of the second generation's central Holocaust icons. Brantzche observes:

> We had a cabinet full of empty *yurtsaht* glasses, enough to hold dozens of drinks at a banquet. To me, *yurtsaht* represented yet another Jewish holiday whose celebration was whimsical and whose meaning was indecipherable. I would not have been surprised to learn that no one else on earth knew a thing about this candle, and assumed that my father had designed a new holiday to remind us that we were Jews (133).

The intrusiveness of the Holocaust past on the American present is a constant fact of life for the second generation.

Survivors' stories are, moreover, different in kind from those told by nonwitnessing parents. Yankl Szuster, for example, tells Brantzche that:

> "Twenty-eight years ago today, the Nazis gassed my mother and four sisters," Papa said. He set down the coffee cup. I thought how in a movie Papa's hands would have trembled, but in real life they were steady.
>
> "And?" I asked.
>
> Papa looked me in the eye. "There is no and," he said (134).

Finkelstein's narrative reminds the audience, much in the manner of Rosensaft's observation, that the second generation has an intensely personal relationship to the *Shoah's* continuing impact. In addition to memorial candles and laconic tales, survivors sometimes possess photos of murdered relatives. The preciousness of these photos is seen in Brantzche's comment that her mother kept them in a leather bag because they were "too sacred for an ordinary photo album" (30).

The crucial link between the generations in *Summer Long-a-Coming* is provided by survivors' tales. The Yad Vashem depositions bond the European Jewish past to the American Jewish present. Rukhl and Yankl describe to the interviewer the experiences and reflections they concealed from their own children. The mother hid in barns and forests for two years while the father was both in a slave labor camp and in hiding. Neither one understands the *Shoah* or attempts to account for the catastrophe theologically. Their response is instead one of faith. Yankl summarizes their belief:

> You ask me why I believe in God, how I can still *daven* to Him three times a day in light of the senseless destruction of my family. You know, you can start out at point "A" and head off in twenty-five different directions. You can wander down strange roads for years, but eventually you have to come back to who you were—to who you are. I believe in God because I have no one else to believe in (182).

Yankl concludes this portion of his testimony with the direct assertion that "My mother and father were Jews and I don't know how to be anything else." This position bears striking similarlity to the epigraph in Wiesel's *A Jew Today* where he records the saying of his Grandfather Dodye Feig, a disciple of the Wishnitzer Rebbe. "You are Jewish," said the grandfather to his young grandson, "your task is to remain Jewish. The rest is up to God."[16]

The father's adherence to traditional beliefs exemplifies the stance adopted by post-Holocaust mainstream orthodox Judaism. Rabbi Eliezer Berkovits, an articulate and erudite nonwitness, is the best known exemplar of this view. He contends, for example, that while the *Shoah* was an enormous human tragedy, theologically it is unexceptional. The catastrope of European Judaism does not alter, modify, or cancel Judaism's millennial messianic belief.[17] Brantzche, however, cannot accept this theological position. Her anger with God is overwhelming. Far from exonerating the divine, Brantzche is convinced that both the Holocaust and her younger sister's death—which she terms "an extension" of the Holocaust—indict God. Brantzche's theological position is reminiscent of Hugh Nissenson's short story "The Blessing."[18] Nissenson tells the tale of Yitshaak, an Israeli whose eight-year old son's life has been claimed by cancer. The father is unable to understand the faith of his survivor aunt who, upon learning of the child's death, recites "Blessed art Thou O Lord who art the true judge in Israel," the traditional benediction on hearing evil news. The difference between the Israeli and the European survivor is that her faith had "taken . . . the condemnation of innocence . . . into account." The survivor's faith, in both the short story and the novel, refuses to be shattered by historical events. It is stronger than the skeptic's doubt.

Finkelstein's Brantzche begins to comprehend her Holocaust legacy following her sister's death. It is only after experiencing this trauma that she can begin to fathom the meaning of unwarranted suffering. Brantzche in fact offers what may be termed a child of survivors philosophy of survival. Her observation deserves full citation:

> Up until that moment, my parents' tales of survival had done little more than fuel my self-emancipation fantasies of entrapment and escape. At best, staying alive was a question of odds, of monitoring the whereabouts of a predator, and side-stepping it in the nick of time. With Perel gone, I had the sickening realization that survival meant coming out the victor by chance, not by destiny or individual cunning. The Szusters were merely like the other creatures on the farm—chickens, earthworms, dogs—who, on suspending their vigilance for a second, succumbed to a greater, more confident power (203–204).

Brantzche's former innocence, i.e., the feeling that she could escape the tenuousness of the human condition, has begun to be replaced by a sober maturity. She now realizes the common human vulnerability uniting her with her parents. Her unwitting experience of tragedy sensitizes Brantzche to the depths of the evil. She begins to understand, for example, that Jews were murdered not for anything they did, but because they had been born. There was, moreover, no escaping the bureaucracy of murder which was everywhere abetted by an omnipresent anti-Semitism. Brantzche's mature assumption of her identity as a daughter of survivors is seen in her faithful auditing of the tapes of her parents' depositions, sent to her by another survivor.

By the novel's end, Brantzche Szuster is a young adult seeking to formulate the specific elements of her identity as a daughter of Holocaust survivors. Listening to her parents' tapes has compelled Brantzche's realization that the *Shoah's* meaning would forever elude her: "I was thrown into despair," she confides, "because I realized I had never understood anything. Certainly, I had never known who Rukhl and Yankl Szuster were." Nevertheless, Brantzche, much in the manner of Wiesel's characters, attempts to transform despair into creativity. In an action characteristic of survivors' children, she reads Holocaust literature vociferously. Realizing that she is unspeakably different from her parents, Brantzche nonetheless identifies a crucial link between the first and second generations. She writes:

> Like them, I live without hope of settling scores yet love life unreasonably,
> and will until the day I die—even though I cannot reclaim what I have
> lost (262).

This insight, won through the pain of personal experience, distinguishes
works written by children of survivors from those of nonwitnessing
writers.

Finkelstein's novel appears to hold a dim view of the Jewish future
in America. A friend of the Szuster family, also the son of survivors,
marries, divorces, and remarries a non-Jewish woman. Brantzche
herself is unmarried. She observes, moreover, that America seems
unsuited to the task of preserving memory. "Qualities like Moma
and Papa's fortitude and patience were "dispensable values here, like
memory . . . outdated and ineffective in an age of time-saving,
convenience commodities" (301). Yet the author herself counsels not
despair but determination to keep alive memory of the Holocaust.

UNIVERSALISTIC

Julie Salamon, film critic for *The Wall Street Journal*, is the daughter
of Holocaust survivors who tried to protect their children from
knowledge of the *Shoah's* horrors. In an interview she commented on
the relationship of the *Shoah* to second generation Jewish identity.
Unlike Finkelstein, Salamon sees the catastrophe not as a shadow,
but as an overwhelming presence. "The Holocaust," Salamon observed,
"is so primal, especially for somebody whose parents are survivors.
It's at the core of your being."[19] Finkelstein and Salamon, however,
attempt to wrest meaning from the disaster." Finkelstein focuses on
psychological and theological issues; Salamon emphasizes what she
perceives to be the *Shoah's* societal legacy. This legacy is nothing less
than "a cry for Justice" emanating from the ovens of Auschwitz. This
cry, although a nomative component of the Jewish tradition, especially
in its prophetic manifestation, assumes an unprecedented post-Holocaust intensity.

In her novel, *White Lies*, Salamon comes to terms with her second
generation identity while attempting to define the relationship of the
Holocaust to American culture.[20] The novels' 24 chapters deal with
the life of Jamaica Just, a features reporter for a newspaper whose
managing editor—a thoroughly assimilated Jew—criticizes her for
insisting on "taking everything so personally" (102). Throughout the
novel there are frequent references to Jamaica's attempt to "right the
world's wrongs, or even to understand them" (106). It surely is not
accidental in this context that the hardcover is engraved with the

image of a Don Quixote figure. (By contrast, the image on the dustjacket of Finkelstein's book is one of sheep being led, presumably to slaughter.) There is as well the symbolism of her last name. Just, the name of her father's European birthplace, was given to the immigration officials by Jamaica's mother. "Just, in English," observes her mother, "carried with it such a noble meaning" (35). Jamaica is, therefore, not only a Just, she searches for Justice.

Jamaica views her writing assignments as "crusades for betterment." Her stories reflect the range of America's urban landscape with its random violence, its impersonal nature, and its persistent forms of racial and religious hatreds. Three of these stories frame Jamaica's personal narrative, putting second generation issues in sharp focus. She writes a piece on second generation teenage welfare mothers, one on children of Holocaust survivors, and a feature story on the so-called "news junkies"—compulsive writers of letters to the editor. These stories are, in the final analysis, interrelated and mutually illuminating. The second generation of welfare mothers is, for example, symbolically linked to the second generation of Holocaust survivors. One of the news junkies, Jules Marlin, is himself a Holocaust survivor with surprising pre-Holocaust links to Jamaica's father. Through these, and other, episodes the reader learns of Jamaica's childhood in a rural Ohio town where hers was the only Jewish family, the kindness and anger of her now deceased physician father, her mother's inventiveness in concealing the truth of the *Shoah* from her daughters while protecting her husband from their children's emotional intrusions, the differences between survivor families and American Jews, and the *Shoah's* continuing trauma.

White Lies presents a sensitive portrayal of the second generation's complex relationship to the *Shoah*. Jamaica's anxieties concerning this relationship are renewed when she is assigned to write about her experience. Reflecting on the fact that she had spent years "anguishing over this pivotal event of her life, and the fact that it had taken place before she'd been born," Jamaica feels doubly alienated. She was not only "untimely born," but also cut off from other Jews "who were made uncomfortable by the ugly scar on her past" (33). But had anything really happened to her? Her memories of the Holocaust really consisted only of the stories she had heard from her parents. And they, like many survivors, preferred not to speak intimately about their ordeal. They, observes Jamaica, "did not belong to the Jules Marlin survivors school, with the clearly defined 'Never Forget!' as their rallying cry" (33). Her parents wanted the world to remember their ordeal, but they attempted to shield their children from the past. In order to further this goal, Jamaica's mother, Eva, fabricated stories about the past. Explaining the novel's title, Jamaica muses about Eva: "she wasn't a liar," but "a woman of imagination." In any case, Jamaica had no choice but to accept the assignment; "she wanted to forget but it was her birthright to remember. Lucky her, Chosen of the Chosen" (28).

But if Jamaica's relationship to the *Shoah* is, like that of Brantzche Szuster, both intensely personal and at a remove, her relationship to American Jewry is more clearly defined. For example, when she first meets Sammy, her future husband, they are amazed at the many things they have in common: "close families, energy, and, perhaps above all, Jewishness, a shared heritage" (33). But the differing nature of this Jewishness illustrates the chasm separating survivors and their children from nonwitnessing families. Sammy's parents, for example, spent the war years on a Texas Air Force base. The recollections of that time, which they shared with their children, were encapsulated by humorous anecdotes. Jamaica, on the other hand, has different memories of the war. She recalls having believed for most of her childhood that "all parents of Jewish children spent World War II in concentration camps or in hiding" (34).

Children of survivors seem, incidentally, to learn of the *Shoah* in a variety of ways, most of them informal in nature. Helen Epstein notes this phenomenon among the children of survivors with whom she spoke. All of those interviewed, writes Epstein,

> said they had absorbed their parents' attitudes toward Germany and the Holocaust experience through a kind of wordless osmosis. They had not been explicitly instructed to feel one way or another. Rather, they had picked up on cues, attitudes, desires that had never been expressed in words.[21]

To return to *White Lies:* The Holocaust was "one of those vague facts we (her older sister and herself) knew about our parents, like the fact that our mother grew up in an unknowable—and unspellable— place called Berecszacz" (34). Consequently, despite their superficial affinity, Jamaica and Sammy, both born after the *Shoah*, are separated by their different relationships to the destruction of European Judaism. As the novel unfolds, in fact, it is Jamaica's second generation legacy; a passion for Justice coupled with her own personal feelings of inadequacy that result in a marital crisis.

Jamaica Just, like Brantzche Szuster, spends her youth surrounded by non-Jews. As the town's only physician, however, her father was a central communal figure. But the Justs remained social and religious outsiders, the town's "glamorous oddballs." Certain psychic landmarks stand out on Jamaica's path to recognizing the *Shoah's* second generation legacy. Once, for example, in the fifth grade her "only partly anti-Semitic" teacher asked the class to trace their genealogy. When the young girl asked her father about their family tree, Dr. Just responded cryptically, "Ours has been pruned." Undeterred, Jamaica copied her teacher's family tree, "leafy with ancestry," and could not understand why, when she showed it to Eva, her mother began to cry. Both of these events underscore Epstein's point about the nonverbal manner by which survivors sometimes transmit their Holocaust experience. Shortly after this incident, Jamaica recalls becoming virulently anti-German, refusing even to eat German chocolate cake.

Jamaica's second generation identity comes to stronger light, however, as she gets older. Unlike Brantzche, Jamaica attends college and it is there that she begins to define the distinctiveness of her legacy. She becomes physically upset when, in Jerzy Kosinski's *The Painted Bird*, reading about "the Jews going to slaughter." Jamaica offers both a counter interpretation of, and a wrenching personal midrash on, the *Shoah's* meaning for the second generation. She writes:

> Those Jews aren't nameless, pitiable beings to me, yesterday's swollen bellies, a 40-year-old newsmagazine cover. They are my mother, my father, my uncles, my aunts, my cousins. They are me (37).

The second generation knows that the Holocaust involved people, not numbers. Moreover, this generation views itself as the continuors of an identity which had come perilously close to having been completely extinguished. Yet in attempting to compose her story, Jamaica is confronted with the problematic nature of her task. The *Shoah* defies meaning as it defies language itself. One cannot write, and yet at the same time one must write. Jamaica laments the *Shoah's* commercialization; recalling survivor gatherings which featured T shirts printed with "I survived Auschwitz." Simultaneously, however, she feels compelled to testify. Her attitude exemplifies the dialectical tension between speech and silence which Wiesel points to as characteristic in authentic witnesses.[22]

Jamaica's determination to warn humanity compels her to enunciate the *Shoah's* universal lessons. In a long meditation, she speaks of these lessons she herself learned by being a child of survivors, and in singular fashion enunciates her consequent legacy to the third generation. Her words deserve full citation.

> I want my children, when I have them, to know what happened during World War II. I don't want them to think their birthright is privilege

and ease. I hope they have those things. I have. But I want them to
know that such things are a matter of luck and circumstances and
should be appreciated. My Mother, too, was a child of privilege for
the first eighteen years of her life. I guess I will make my children
feel guilty, even though that isn't my intent (44).

It is not guilt, however, that Jamaica wishes to instill. Rather, it is
social responsibility or, better yet, mature civic virtue. This desire
emerges from her reading of the disaster's universal lessons. She wants
her yet unborn children

to learn what I think I've learned. I make an effort to be decent because
I have some understanding of what happens when decency doesn't
exist. I try to keep aware of what the government is doing because I
have some understanding of what happens when governments turn
evil. I try to be good to my family and friends because I have some
understanding of what it's like to have family and friends taken away.

Jamaica concludes her reflection by making a distinction which has
crucial bearing on what second generation literature is. And what it
is not. "Most of all," she writes, "I understand that I have only some
understanding of these things, which is quite different from experience."
Children of survivors do have a personal relationship to the *Shoah's*
continuing effect. But as Brantzche discovered, there is an enormous
distinction between the children and their parents.

Jamaica's parents, unlike the Szusters, are secular Jews. Yet her
father, Dr. Pearlman, insists on raising his daughters Jewishly. He
personifies the experience of many prewar secularists for whom the
Shoah provided their point of entry into Jewish history.[23] In fact, later
in the novel Jamaica learns that the Jews in pre-Holocaust Just
"identified with their urbane coreligionists in Germany rather than
the ghettoized Jews of Eastern Europe." From this information Jamaica,
like Brantzche, realizes that all Europe's Jews were doomed. Birth
itself was a death sentence. Dr. Perlman's nurturing of his children's
Jewish identity is, however, a complex matter. On the one hand, he
brought them a comic book version of the Hebrew bible with accompanying records, and encouraged his wife to light Friday night
candles in order, attests Jamaica, that "our Presbyterian surrounding
wouldn't obliterate the yellow stars engraved on our souls." But Dr.
Perlman always encouraged his daughters to think of themselves as
Americans first, and gave them money when they went on dates so
that they would not be dependent on anyone. Eva, for her part, in

one breath both reminds her daughters to light *yizkor* (memorial) candles for their murdered relatives, and calls her stockbroker.

White Lies, much in the manner of *Summer Long-a-Coming*, tells of a traumatic death which both initiates a member of the second generation into the mystery of theodicy and reveals the vulnerability of the human condition. Jamaica recalls, for example, the traumatic death of her highschool friend who died in an auto accident. In mourning, she repeats Jeremiah's question of why the innocent suffer. Eva responds by referring to her camp experience and, in the process, displays aspects of what Robert Jay Lifton terms "psychic numbing." Concerning the death of the innocent, for example, Eva contends, "I never feel like I'm part of it. In that camp I felt like I was floating above it all, like I wasn't there" (179). She concludes by telling her daughter that one did not see the dead in Auschwitz. Rather, "one could smell them" as they burned in the crematorium.

Jamaica next turns to her seriously ill father with the same query. The physician, although not religious, replies in the traditional manner by contending that God's ways cannot be explained. Pushed by his daughter whether he himself believed in God, Dr. Perlman first responds with a kind of Aristotelian "Unmoved Mover" assertion which his daughter, who like all teenagers is searching for something more personal and reassuring, rejects. In response to her momentary fatalism, Dr. Perlman tells Jamaica that one must do one's best on earth and not be concerned about heaven or divine forgiveness. More in despair than ever, she again asks if he believes in God. Unwilling to confess his disbelief, he now replies that one must learn that death is part of life, and that her dead friend had just learned this lesson "a little early." Jamaica is outraged by his apparent lack of sensitivity and asks whether her father's callousness stems from the fact that since her friend was not Jewish, he was not good enough to care about. Later, Jamaica's universalism will be thoroughly grounded in her Jewishness. It is as if she had adopted Wiesel's position that the Holocaust's uniqueness resides in its Jewish specificity.[24]

Jamaica has two sources of information about the Holocaust; one is cognitive and comes from her voracious reading on the topic. This is a commonly reported phenomenon in second generation literature. Novels by Friedmann, Finkelstein, Spiegelman, and others all refer to their authors' immersion in books about the *Shoah*. The other source, survivors' tales which she hears from her mother and Jules Marlin, is both affective and cognitive in nature; these tales rivet their auditor. From her mother Jamaica learns of the cruel logic which ruled the kingdom of night. Eva, for example, contends that the infamous Dr. Mengele saved her life. Pushed by her daughter on the meaning of this astounding assertion, Eva acknowledges that Mengele chose her to live and sent her mother, Jamaica's grandmother, to the gas. But, attests Eva, this was a favor for her own mother never would have survived. Eva also recounts the tale of a particularly cruel "selection" in which a healthy young Jewish woman was sent to her death. Within one week the victim's mother died and her sister went mad. That, confides Eva, was when she began hating Mengele. These tales from the kingdom of night are reported while mother and daughter are waiting for a tennis court to become available, thereby merging the Holocaust past and post-Holocaust America. Eva's testimony is delivered, moreover, in the same tone of voice with which she used to talk about her friends' husbands' business problems or to complain about her own tennis serve. That the horror is recounted in a matter of fact manner, much like Brantzche Szuster's father recalling the gassing of his mother and four sisters, serves in both cases to heighten the tragedy's incomprehensibility.

Jews who survived the Holocaust did so in a variety of ways. Jules smuggled himself on to a train and, after leaving Just, hid in a cellar which he shared with a young Jewish couple and their child. His story also reveals the existence of the righteous among the gentiles. Jules survived owing to the help of two Christians. His story illustrates the bizarre combination of overwhelming Christian anti-Semitism and the few cases of altruistic behavior among Europe's non-Jewish World War II population. But Jamaica learns more from Jules. He, like her father, was an enlightened Jew, who had gone to a public school rather than a religious one. For the Nazis, however, such distinctions were meaningless. All Jews were to be exterminated. The fact that Jules had also planned to become a physician illustrates again how the *Shoah*, when it did not take lives, forever damaged them. Jules came from the same city as her parents and his brother had been Dr. Perlman's best friend. Jules had been in love with her father's first wife; a beautiful woman who along with her infant daughter had been gassed at Auschwitz. This revelation simultaneously explains her father's periodic rages and the frequent arguments between her parents, in Hungarian, the intensity of which had, as a little girl, frightened her into hiding in the closet. The emotional weight of murdered siblings is borne by their post-Auschwitz half-brothers and sisters.[25]

Jules and Jamaica also share a passion for justice. Jules' indefatigable letter writing reveals his great concern for a society which is morally adrift. Both he and Jamaica exemplify what Wiesel has termed "mystical madness,"[26] the determination to care in a world characterized by indifference and mendacity. Reactions to her Holocaust article had, for example, revealed that readers were for the most part tired of hearing about it. Near the end of the novel Jamaica summarizes why Jules, and she herself, seem odd to the rest of the world. It is, she attests, "only because you are still capable of feeling outrage" (247). This observation calls to mind Wiesel's statement that in the early days he used to shout in order to change man. Now, however, he contends that he shouts in order to prevent man from ultimately changing him.[27] For Jamaica this endless shout is compelled by her knowledge that the world is not yet redeemed. Viewing the world through a Holocaust prism, she dislikes unfairness and all forms of social injustice: anti-Semitism, poverty, racism. The difference between her and her husband is, for example, that she contends the glass is half empty, whereas for Sammy it is half full.

Jamaica's universalizing of the *Shoah's* lessons is, however, seen most clearly in her concern for second generation welfare mothers. Welfare epitomizes poverty's unfairness which, thinks Jamaica, is only made worse by government meddling. Accepting the assignment, Jamaica wants to write about an individual "bravely trying to fight the system." But she is also motivated by personal reasons, identifying with Lonnie—the young mother about whom she writes. Jamaica is explicit on this point, telling Sammy that:

> It's hard to explain. I guess I have this image of myself as a martyr once removed, that somehow I've been victimized by the Holocaust even though that was my parents' show, not mine. In a weird way, I guess I "related" to Lonnie, stuck where she is because of her parents (71).

Jamaica confides to the reader, moreover, that the "mere thought of sadness—anyone's sadness—made her chest ache and her eyes water with sympathetic congestion" (167). She is attuned, in other words, to life's so-called little things. In this regard it is instructive to recall the passage in *Night* where Wiesel tells of his father's initial reaction to the decree ordering Jews to wear the yellow star: "Oh well, what of it? You don't die of it." "Poor Father!" exclaims Wiesel, "of what then did you die?"

Jamaica's moral sensitivity extends as well to cerebral concerns. She is, for example, determined not to sink into the anomie that engulfs her generation. This observation includes the distinctive type of literature which her peers are reading. Jamaica shares with the reader the fact that her editor deleted "all of her ideas on the subject from an acerbic piece she'd done on postmodernist fiction, of which he was a great fan." Postmodernist fiction is a cipher for the ethically unanchored life and Jamaica is painfully aware of cultural fads which easily lend themselves to fascist ways of thought and behavior. It is precisely this type of literature which revels in abandoning a pursuit for moral responsibility. Jamaica is well aware of the fact that it was, after all, intellectuals and university trained people who organized and planned the Holocaust.

White Lies has an appropriately ambiguous conclusion. Jamaica's marriage is failing at least in part because her husband cannot cope with his wife's intensity and concern which, he feels, leave no room for their own relationship. On the other hand, Jamaica's relationship with her mother and sister is, if anything, stronger at novel's end. Both sisters work for the betterment of humanity, Jamaica through her writing and sense of compassion, while her older sister Geneva is a physician. Jamaica displays a secular messianism which is expressed in her concern for others; a concern which corresponds to what both Porter and Savran/Fogelman observed in their work with adult children of survivors.[28] In this context it is important to note that *White Lies* compares clinical understandings of survivors to the personal knowledge of the second generation. Jamaica is opposed to psychiatrists and to psychologists. But Geneva, who like Art Spiegelman had a troubled relationship to Judaism, sought psychotherapy. Her analyst views the Justs as victims rather than as people. A psychologist analyzes Jules Marlin's letter writing as a harmless form of "undoing," more neurotic than psychotic. Neither of these professionals has really understood either the survivor phenomenon or the messages these people have. Despite the obstacles and the indifference, Jamaica cannot and will not abandon her Holocaust driven desire to improve the world.

CONCLUSION

This brief survey leads to several conclusions about second generation Holocaust literature. Theologically, this writing is a primary example of what Greenberg designates "new secular liturgical acts" which respond to the Holocaust while revealing that its authors have, despite God's apparent hiddeness and reluctance to act, refused to abandon covenantal Judaism. In literary terms, there is now a crucial third type of writing in addition to witnesses and "witnesses through the imagination" that one can turn to for understanding the *Shoah*'s contemporary meaning. These writings are, moreover, important for their sense of moral purpose and mission, reflecting Wiesel's contention that contemporary writers must write with the Holocaust as background, and that the task of the writer is not to entertain but to instruct.[29] While the literary quality of second generation novels is uneven, they play an incalculably important role as testimony written by those who seek the parameters of authentic post-Auschwitz Judaism. The *Shoah* in these writings is not a metaphor, nor is it trivialized, amplified, or denied. What is more, this generation has written of the tragedy employing images that are uniquely its own. In this sense, these novels resemble Claude Lanzmann's film *Shoah: An Oral History.* Both genres are able to invoke the unspeakable without utilizing piles of corpses or mounds of hair. Moreover, in terms of the dynamic of Jewish American culture, the writings of this generation seriously undermine the claims of those within the Jewish community who contend that too much attention is paid to the Holocaust or that the *Shoah* is really not the business of the Jews of America.[30]

It surely is not accidental that both novels discussed here employ a traumatic death as a cipher for confronting the suffering of innocents. In psychosocial terms, it is significant that both Brantzche and Jamaica think themselves unworthy. This phenomenon is well attested in survivor families. Stanley L. Rustin, for example, observes that, "The need to accomplish, to please one's parents, is frequently accompanied by excessive anxiety regarding failure or acute guilt if one fails or disappoints one's parents."[31] This feeling of unworthiness stems as well from the offsprings' assumption that they, unlike their parents, could not have survived the Holocaust. Curiosity and even a strange form of jealousy about their parents' survival is another element of second generation literature. Frequently this curiosity is triggered by mundane thoughts about personal hygiene. Both Brantzche Szuster and Jamaica Just, for example, wonder what their mothers used for toilet paper in the camps. The novels of Finkelstein and Salamon, and others like them, herald the appearance of a distinctive second generation literature which, while differing from the witnessing generations' ways of remembering, testify to both the pain and the hope of post-Holocaust Jewish existence.

The lack of overt reference to God in second generation literature should be equated neither with theological denial nor indifference. Rather, this literature, as we have seen, confirms Greenberg's insight concerning the nature of the voluntary covenant. All who voluntarily live a Jewish life, he contends, voluntarily embrace the covenant and thereby express an "affirmation of God's presence."[32] This literature can thus be viewed as expressing a new stage in affirming the covenant and chosenness. The post-Auschwitz affirmation, however, is etched by memories of growing up in homes where the *Shoah's* continuing impact, although expressed in a variety of ways, was experienced as a great hovering presence. Second generation Holocaust literature displays a concern for the issues of Jewish identity and possesses a moral urgency which reveal profoundly the understanding that the ashes of the Holocaust will forever be intermingled with the hope of its survivors and their descendants.

NOTES

1. Irving Abrahamson, *ed.*, *Against Silence: The Voice and Vision of Elie Wiesel.* New York: Holocaust Library, 1985, vol. 3, p. 324.

2. Alvin H. Rosenfeld, *A Double Dying: Reflections On Holocaust Literature.* Bloomington, Ind.: Indiana University Press, 1980, p. 19.

3. Irving Greenberg, *The Voluntary Covenant.* New York: CLAL-National Jewish Resource Center, 1982, p. 11.

4. Norma Rosen, "The Second Life of Holocaust Imagery." *Midstream,* New York. vol. 33, no. 4, Apr. 1987.

5. *Ibid.*, p. 58.

6. On the theme of readers becoming witnesses see Ellen Fine's excellent book *Legacy of Night: The Literary Universe of Elie Wiesel.* Albany, NY: SUNY Press, 1982.

7. Norma Rosen, "The Holocaust and the American Jewish Novelist." *Midstream,* New York, vol. 20, no. 8, Oct. 1974.

8. Concerning the sacrality of witness testimony see the following works: Eliezer Berkovits, *Faith After The Holocaust.* New York: KTAV, 1973, p. 78. Irving Greenberg, *The Voluntary Covenant.* p. 27. Primo Levi, *Survival in Auschwitz.* Translated by S. Woolf. New York: Collier Books, 1961, p. 59. The essays of Elie Wiesel, especially his remarks in "Jewish Values in the Post-Holocaust Future: A Symposium." *Judaism,* vol. 16, no. 3, Summer 1967, p. 285.

9. Menachem Rosensaft, "Reflections of a Child of Holocaust Survivors." *Midstream,* New York, vol. 27, no. 9, Nov. 1981, p. 31.

10. Jack Nusan Porter, "Is There a Survivor's Syndrome? Psychological and Socio-Political Implications." *Confronting History and Holocaust: Collected Essays.* Lanham, MD: University Press of America, 1983, pp. 100–104.

11. Bela Savran and Eva Fogelman, "Psychological Issues in the Lives of Children of Holocaust Survivors: The Children as Adults." in Lucy Y. Steinitz and David M. Szony, *eds.*, *Living After the Holocaust: Reflections by Children of Survivors in America.* New York: Bloch Publishing Company, 1979, p. 152.

12. *Ibid.*

13. Barbara Finkelstein, Lecture at Syracuse University. Oct. 5, 1987.

14. *Ibid.*

15. Barbara Finkelstein, *Summer Long-a-Coming.* New York: Harper & Row, 1987. Page numbers from this novel appear in parentheses.

16. Elie Wiesel, *A Jew Today.* Translated by Marion Wiesel. New York: Vintage Books, 1979. Epigraph.

17. For an analysis of Berkovits' views, see Alan L. Berger, "Holocaust and History: A Theological Reflection." *Journal of Ecumenical Studies*, vol. 25, no. 2, Spring 1988. pp. 203–205, and 207–208.

18. Hugh Nissenson, "The Blessing" in his *A Pile of Stones*. New York: Charles Scribner's Sons, 1965. For further study of this story see Alan L. Berger, *Crisis and Covenant: The Holocaust in American Jewish Fiction*. Albany, NY: SUNY Press, 1985, chapter 3.

19. Alexander Wohl, "Interview with Julie Salamon." *Baltimore Jewish Times*, Feb. 19, 1988, p. 60.

20. Julie Salamon, *White Lies*. Boston: Hill & Company, 1987. Page numbers from this novel appear in parentheses.

21. Helen Epstein, *Children of the Holocaust: Conversations with Sons and Daughters of Survivors*. New York: G. P. Putman's Sons, 1979, p. 137.

22. This is a central part of Wiesel's work. An especially succinct statement appears in Lily Edelman's "A Conversation with Elie Wiesel" in Harry James Cargas, *ed., Responses to Elie Wiesel*. New York: Persea Books, 1978, pp. 9–22.

23. On this point see A. L. Berger, *Crisis and Covenant*, chapter 4, "Judaism as a Secular Value System."

24. Wiesel's most pointed comments on the relationship of the unique to the universal occur in his remarks as Chairman of the United States Holocaust Council. His most dramatic statement of Holocaust particularly is seen in his aphorism that while "not all victims were Jews, all Jews were victims." Abrahamson, *Against Silence: The Voice and Vision of Elie Wiesel*. p. 172. But the *Shoah*'s universal implications can be seen only through its Jewish specificity. The United States Holocaust Memorial Museum is in fact, attests Wiesel, to serve as a universal early warning system. The Protestant theologian Robert McAfee Brown thoughtfully captures the essence of Wiesel's view in writing "through them (the Jewish victims) and beyond them but not without them." Robert McAfee Brown, *Elie Wiesel: Messenger To All Humanity*. Notre Dame, IN: University of Notre Dame Press, 1983, p. 137.

25. This is the case in Thomas Friedmann's *Damaged Goods;* Elie Wiesel's *The Fifth Son* (1985), a novel about the second generation; and Art Spiegelman's *Maus*. For a detailed study of the first two novels see Alan L. Berger, "Memory and Meaning: The Holocaust in Second Generation Literature" in Zev Garber, Alan L. Berger, and Richard Libowitz, eds. *Methodology in the Academic Teaching of the Holocaust*. Laham, MD: University Press of America, 1988, pp. 177–181. On *The Fifth Son* see Berger, *Crisis and Covenant*, pp. 68–79. For an analysis of Spiegelmann's book see Berger, "Bearing Witness: Second Generation Literature of the Shoah" in *Remembering for the Future: Working Papers*. Oxford: Pergamon Press, 1988, pp. 22–31.

26. Abrahamson, *Against Silence: The Voice and Vision of Elie Wiesel*. vol. 3, p. 232.

27. Elie Wiesel, *One Generation After*. New York: Schocken Books, 1982, p. 72.

28. See above, footnotes 10 and 11.

29. Abrahamson, *Against Silence: The Voice and Vision of Elie Wiesel.* vol. 1, p. 15.

30. For an analysis and critique of these views see Berger, "Holocaust and History: A Theological Reflection." See especially pp. 205–211.

31. Stanley L. Rustin, "The Post-Holocaust Generations." in Randolph L. Braham, *ed., Perspectives on the Holocaust.* Boston: Kluwer Nihoff Publishing, 1983, p. 37.

32. Greenberg, *The Voluntary Covenant.* p. 21.

Fictional Facts and Factual Fictions: History in Holocaust Literature

Lawrence L. Langer

I call this essay fictional facts and factual fictions in order to suggest a symbiotic kinship between actual and imaginative truth in the literature of the Holocaust. One of the many tasks of Holocaust criticism is to clarify the complex bond, in the minds of both author and audience, linking the oppressions of history to the impressions of art. Normally, the artist is free, and indeed expected, to manipulate reality in any way his vision sees fit. The imagination seizes experience, drops it into its crucible, allows it to ferment, and offers the results to a tolerant and often eager public. Few readers today fault Tolstoy's art for being "unfair" to Napoleon in *War and Peace*, any more than they censure Hawthorne for adapting Puritan values to the needs of his theme in various stories and novels. But Rolf Hochhuth roused a storm of controversy when he dramatized the "facts" of Pope Pius XII's attitude toward the Jews, thus making of it a fictional fact that forced audiences to acknowledge the tension between actual and imagined truth. Similarly, in *King of the Jews*, Leslie Epstein antagonized many by transforming the "facts" of Chaim Rumkowski's leadership in the Lodz ghetto into the extravagant antics of I.C. Trumpelman. Somehow, they felt, the imagined tone of comedy and farce seemed inappropriate to the actual details of the atrocity it sought to illuminate. The same, of course, has been said repeatedly of Lina Wertmüller's film *Seven Beauties*, which offends the memory and sensibilities of viewers who anticipate greater fidelity to the realities of the concentration camp ordeal.

When the Holocaust is the theme, history imposes limitations on the supposed flexibility of artistic license. We are confronted by the perplexing challenge of the reversal of normal creative procedure: instead of Holocaust fictions liberating the facts and expanding the range of their implications, Holocaust facts enclose the fictions, drawing

the reader into an ever narrower area of association, where history
and art stand guard over their respective territories, wary of abuses
that either may commit upon the other.

The problem is not exclusively the reader's or author's. Essentially,
the problem is time's, and eventually time will solve it. What will
happen, for example, when the specific details of the atrocities at
Babi Yar and Auschwitz are forgotten, when their associations with
the Holocaust have passed beyond historical memory and they become
mere place names as obscure to their audiences as Borodino and
Tagliamento are to Tolstoy's and Hemingway's readers today? In time,
in other words, the boundaries separating the historical moment from
its imaginative rendition will be blurred, and it will no longer matter
so much whether fictional facts, tied to the actual deeds of history,
have become factual fictions, monuments to artistic vision that require
no defense or justification, but stand or fall on the strength of their
aesthetic mastery of material.

But today it still matters, because the urgency of the historical
event continues to exert its mysterious power over modern consciousness. A fictional Napoleon no longer triggers an alarm, but the
presence of Rudolf Hoess, commandant of Auschwitz, in Willilam
Styron's *Sophie's Choice*, sets off sirens of wary constraint. One admires
the imaginative courage, if not the results, of George Steiner's effort
to write a fiction whose central fact is that Israeli agents have discovered
an aged Adolf Hitler, very much alive, deep in a South American
jungle. Reading that novella, *The Voyage to San Cristobal of A.H.*,
imposes almost impossible burdens on the audience's willing sus-
pension of disbelief, confronted as it is simultaneously with the
historical fact of Hitler's death and his artistic resurrection, a burden
that would be negligible if Steiner's intention were not so serious and
the figure were not so centrally identified with the experience of the
Holocaust. By re-creating a Holocaust personality whose motives still
have not been firmly established (to say nothing of being understood)
in *fact*, Steiner establishes a wall of resistance to block the passage
leading from history to art. Once the historical Hitler becomes a
fictional fact, he inadvertently joins the fraternity of men; then (since
his creator eschews melodrama), we are forced to face him in fiction
as we were reluctant to do in fact. The factual fiction, in other words,
becomes a figure we do not want to confront, partly because the real
man is still so much more vivid to our imagination than his invented
counterpart, and partly because the fact and the fiction constantly
war with each other for higher priority. The Holocaust in fact resists
displacement by the Holocaust in fiction, as if the artist were guilty
of some unprincipled violation of a sacred shrine. This may help to

explain Adorno's early cry, constantly repeated by others though later modified by him, that to write poetry after Auschwitz is barbaric.

How may we account for this resistance? If the Holocaust were an event that lent itself to heroic portraiture, or the legendary tone of epic, or even to the conventional tale of purification through suffering— and of course much Holocaust literature limits itself to expressing just such traditional themes—then this problem, I think, would not exist. Literature generalizes human experience, while the events of atrocity we call the Holocaust insist on their singularity. The imagination seeks to link the two, to find a bridge through metaphor, image, a language of connection. But the Holocaust has impurified language in a way that prevents this from happening. Norma Rosen quotes a line from a poem by Eugene Montale—"I've sniffed on the wind the burnt fragrance/of sweet rolls from the ovens"—and suggests that no one today can register those images without some form of associative despair.[1] The catalogue of such terms is long, and if they do not deplete available vocabulary, they certainly limit the writer's control of their use: train, track, boxcar, smoke, chimney, ghetto, roundup, deport, roll call, organize, camp, block, oven, furnace, gas, shower— even arrival and departure. They are not a lingo (though some unique terms like kapo and musselman and Canada appeared, with many more emerging from the longer Gulag experience that Solzhenitsyn writes of), but ordinary language that normally empowers the writer to give rebirth in literature to the tensions and conflicts of life.

How do we verbalize the enigma of a language that alienates even as it struggles to connect? We can avoid the problem, as many do, by choosing a language of consolation and transforming the Holocaust experience into a story of Jewish resistance and survival, pretending that these terms at least permit the universalization of the ordeal. But those who confront that ordeal with unabashed frankness will have to acknowledge that in its scope it was little more than, and never *will* be much more than a story of Jewish murder. Since the *factual* fact is so dismal and unedifying, how are we to face the fictional fact that lifts it out of its original bedrock in history (where, four decades later, we still probe for its "meanings" in the layers of time), and translates it into an artificial setting? How can we expect the mind to adjust from the real horror to its portrayal in art, while simultaneously accepting the premise that nothing essential has been lost or changed in the process?

Sometimes I think this is too much to ask, of writer *or* audience. Except for the brief episode near the end of André Schwarz-Bart's *Last of the Just*, I know of no fictional moment set *inside* a gas chamber (though probably others exist). Making a fictional fact of that factual fact raises the specter of the resultant factual fiction's becoming "only" a fictional fiction, by which I mean that for the sake of art, the imagination raises the event to the level of imagined experience and somehow constricts instead of illuminating the implications of that dehumanizing trial. Art in its essence asks us to see life other than it literally was, since all art, even the most objective naturalism, requires selection and composition, and this alters the purity (or in this case the impurity) of the original historical moment. A wholly imagined fictional episode, or one unrelated to a sustained trauma like the Holocaust, faces no such constraints. Hence the temptation is to defer to tradition by heroizing the victim by identifying him or her with familiar forms of suffering and well-known gestures of resistance, or villainizing the persecutor through familiar expressions of cruelty. But these are evasive tactics too.

Another task of Holocaust criticism is to address the implications and consequences of these dilemmas. Some writers are more sensitive to the issue than others. Wishing the life of his heroine in *The White Hotel* to end at Babi Yar, D.M. Thomas—wisely, I think—does not try to reconstruct that episode as a purely imaginative act because he knows, perhaps through instinct, that the Holocaust raises questions of narrative authority few other historical occasions confront us with. Moreover, since the intersection of history with fiction, actual with imaginative truth, is one of the themes of Thomas's novel, introducing a literal eyewitness account of Babi Yar into the text reinforces the issue he is exploring. He takes most of the description of the catastrophe of Babi Yar from Anatoli Kuznetsov's non-fiction novel of the same name. As a young boy, Kuznetsov lived in Kiev and experienced some of the events surrounding the executions at Babi Yar. But even he felt the need for a more reliable narrative authority and, as he tells us, used the account of a survivor, Dina Mironovna Pronicheva. "She is the only eyewitness to come out of it," he says (inaccurately, as it turns out), "and I am now going to tell her story, as I wrote it down from her own words, without adding anything of my own."[2] Curiously, this is a familiar formula to anyone conversant with the history of the novel. Unwilling to be accused of frivolous fabrications, some early novelists habitually fell back on such disclaimers, as if invented narratives would somehow seem less authentic than so-called authoritative testimony. Ironically—for some writers, at any rate—the Holocaust has revived an ancient tradition. Perhaps this accounts for the popularity of one form of Holocaust literature, the documentary novel, represented not only by Kuznetsov's work, but also by Jean-François Steiner's *Treblinka* and Thomas Kenneally's *Schindler's List*.

Thomas's purpose, however, is not to give us an authoritative account of Babi Yar, but to find a fitting dramatic conclusion to the life of his heroine and erstwhile patient of Sigmund Freud, the fictional Lisa Erdmann. The reader, already compelled to identify her character with historical reality by the presence of Freud in the novel, has the merging of her story into fictional fact confirmed by her fate at Babi Yar. "No one could have imagined the scene," she thinks as the executions continue, "because it was happening."[3]

Facts we *know* because they have happened; fictions we only imagine. But the facts of Babi Yar are "unimaginable," and this is why what I call fictional facts play such an important role in our response to and understanding of the Holocaust. By creating an imagined context for Dina Pronicheva's experience at Babi Yar, Thomas makes accessible to the imagination what might have seemed intractable material. But at the same time, he alters the narrative of the real survivor, Dina Pronicheva, whose ordeal is transmitted by Kuzentsov; and in so doing, he creates what I call a factual fiction, since there never was a Lisa Erdmann, so that her "perception" of Babi Yar is an invention. The reader searching for information about or insight into Babi Yar by reading *The White Hotel* runs the same risk as one turning to John Hersey's *The Wall* to learn about the Warsaw ghetto. Art intervenes almost inevitably to mute the impact of history, just as Thomas chose to end his novel with a fantasy that at the very least qualifies the finality of the anguish represented by the real Babi Yar. Although *The White Hotel* is not exclusively a Holocaust novel, the extermination of the Jews is the denouement of its fictional milieu. The concluding fantasy of transcendence, and perhaps of redemption, wholly a product of the imagination, cannot undo the historical horror of the prior episode at Babi Yar. Whether this is the point, or the missed point, of the narrative, each reader must decide in the privacy of his or her critical engagement with the text.

Babi Yar is an episode, a mass execution, perceived through the eyes of a victim, whose own source, we now know, was primarily the testimony of an actual survivor, Dina Pronicheva. In William Styron's *Sophie's Choice* the commandant of Auschwitz, Rudolf Hoess, is a character, with a wife, children, a home, friends, normal desires, while the "episode" of Auschwitz, with its mass executions, forms only the periphery of the narrative. The fictional facts of Hoess's tenure at Auschwitz come from his *Autobiography*, his various war-crimes trial testimonies, and Styron's own visit to the site of the deathcamp. The factual fictions, however, are far more crucial in this work: the motives, the dialogue, the gestures, the portrait not of Commandant Hoess, but of Hoess the private human being, whose

primary task almost incidentally happens to be the construction of
the gas chambers and crematoria of Auschwitz-Birkenau and the
murder of its Jewish inmates. Between one and two million of them
perished there, by his own estimation (though not in the pages of
this novel).

Far more challenging than Sophie's manufactured choice—sending
her daughter to her death in order to save her son (a decision which
any informed reader would know lay beyond the control of Auschwitz's
victims, Jewish or not)—far more challenging than Sophie's choiceless
choice is *Styron's* choice: to assault our historical consciousness of
Hoess the mass murderer with his own conception of Hoess the man,
and to expect the resulting fictional facts to be persuasive. If they
are not—and I think they are not—the fault lies both with Styron
and the tyranny of history, which at this moment in time demands
to know not how decent and polite Hoess might have been when
he wasn't killing Jews and Poles, but how a man otherwise decent
and polite—questionable designations, at best—so effortlessly advanced the cause of genocide.

The factual fictions of Styron's narrative, solely on his own creative
authority, would have us believe that Commandant Hoess might
apologize to Polish prisoner Sophie for violating his promise by failing
to produce her son for her to see. Or that Commandant Hoess,
destroyer of Jews and Poles, would not object to the humiliation of
vowing to that same Polish prisoner, seriously, not ironically: "You
have my assurance and word as a German officer, my word of honor."
Styron's boldness in characterizing Hoess matches Steiner's in un-
covering Hitler "alive" after all these years: but what fresh understanding of Nazi mentality emerges from their imaginative forays? Is
it a revelation that Hoess suffers from migraines; or is exasperated
by bureaucratic interference from Berlin; or that he is beholden to
former Prussian mannerisms; or admires his Arabian stallion's spon-
taneity? In attempting to imagine Hoess as someone other than a
creature of melodrama, a monster of iniquity, Styron has created an
unremarkable figure almost totally dissociated from the deeds that
led to his execution after the war. The consequences of those deeds,
which engage the reader's consciousness with as much energy as the
factual fictions about Hoess in the novel distract it, solicit something
more than the familiar outlines of characterization that Styron offers
us, something akin to the bizarre contradictions that drive the more
complex nature of Nathan.

Literature may not provide sufficient model or inspiration for
personages like Rudolf Hoess, but history compounds the dilemma
by also hemming in Styron, in spite of himself. He cannot approach

Hoess with the same psychological freedom that he does Nathan; yet to do otherwise is to create a wooden creature whose responses in fiction neither illuminate nor are justified by his actions in fact. *Sophie's Choice* is a classic example of the kinship linking the two, constraining instead of freeing the potential for insight inherent in the bond. We cannot say to the reader: take Hoess for what he is, a character in a novel who need not shed light on his real-life prototype. Such a demand would trivialize history, the victims, the critical imagination, the whole macabre enterprise of genocide. But if a character's representational authority does not emerge from the context of the fiction, how are we to respond to him? We return to the intersection of fiction and fact, history and imagination, and that defiant event we call the Holocaust, which the creative faculty will not dismiss but cannot enclose because the limbo it inhabits is shrouded in such uncertain gloom.

Up to this point I have tried to confirm the difficulty, not to say the impossibility, of making a historical figure the center of consciousness in a piece of Holocaust literature. Whether we are thinking of Hitler, Hoess, Chaim Rumkowski, Pope Pius XII, or any other major participant in the catastrophe, the memory of their actual role intrudes on all attempts to dramatize it and erodes the authenticity of their fictional presence. I am convinced that many decades must pass before art will be able to displace memory as the measure of literary success. The most effective Holocaust fictions, like Piotr Rawicz's *Blood from the Sky*, Jorge Semprun's *The Long Voyage*, Tadeusz Borowski's *This Way for the Gas, Ladies and Gentlemen*, Ida Fink's *A Scrap of Time*, and Aharon Appelfeld's various novels, while not ignoring the specific historical context, turn their imaginative beacons on the problem of tone and point of view, angle of vision, centers of consciousness through which the essential atrocity may be filtered. Although fictionalized historical material may alienate the reader, an adequately imagined *invented* center of consciousness can draw him against his will into the net of atrocity, where his own sense of normal reality struggles to escape from the lure. To balance the theoretical discussion in the first part of this essay, I would like to turn now to two texts (one of them, by design, discussed earlier, but with a different emphasis) in order to assess the use of centers of consciousness as bulwarks against the invasion by Holocaust facts of Holocaust fictions.

Although Saul Bellow's *Mister Sammler's Planet* and Styron's *Sophie's Choice* are not Holocaust novels in the sense of some of the aforementioned works, the title figures in both have had their encounters with mass murder and atrocity. Their lives thereafter have been unalterably affected by their ordeals. Mr. Sammler sees himself as a *"past* person," as "a man who had come back," who "had rejoined life,"[4] though moments of his Holocaust ordeal trickle into the present through his own perceiving consciousness at various points in the narrative. He is his own conduit into the foreground of the novel's action, our only source of authority for the history of the Holocaust "then" and its impact during subsequent years on the mind and vision of Sammler the survivor now.

Sophie is a survivor too, though we shall have to ask how her encounter with atrocity differs from Sammler's. By adopting Stingo as his narrator, Styron prevents Sophie from internalizing her experience as Sammler does, thus excluding the reader from direct access to the inner process whereby she adjusts the background of her ordeal in Poland and Auschwitz to the foreground of her postwar years in Brooklyn. Sophie offers us only oral testimony; Stingo is the perceiving consciousness, and as an aspiring writer, he seems less interested, his assertions to the contrary notwithstanding, in the "meaning" of Auschwitz than in the literary re-creation of Sophie's story and the gradual revelation of her "secret"—the choice between her children, imposed on her by a Nazi doctor at Auschwitz. Stingo thus duplicates in his own career as a fledgling writer the conflict between fictional facts and factual fictions that beset Styron as author of *Sophie's Choice.* Unfortunately, his efforts to achieve equilibrium are no more successful than his creator's.

The Holocaust background of *Sophie's Choice* is thus Sophie's Holocaust experience, the anguish of the loss of her children, her friends, her health, her self-esteem. That experience evolves slowly into the foreground of the novel through the strict shaping control of Stingo's consciousness, but the evolution is so often disrupted by discordant or farcical concerns that the link joining background to foreground ultimately shatters, never to be repaired. These eccentric matters include Stingo's obsessive fantasies about a final resting place for his wayward organ; Nathan's brutal, lunatic antics; and Sophie's determination to master the intricacies of American, and particularly Southern, literary rhetoric. To have a Polish immigrant who mistakes the elementary distinction between seersucker and other kinds of suckers diligently poring over Malcolm Cowley's *Portable Faulkner* or the concise novels of Thomas Wolfe is to strain the reader's credulity. As a writer, Stingo is bound and trapped by his literary commitment to create a portrait of Sophie that is more stylized than human, projecting for us his own version of what a southern American writer might have imagined Sophie to be. The novel is less about Sophie's experience in Auschwitz and her encounter with Commandant Hoess than it is about Stingo's unflagging determination to make literature out of them.

Whether Styron had serious or parodistic intentions with Stingo, the results, for readers interested in the uses of Holocaust facts in fiction, are the same. Striving for literary effects turns out to be incompatible with Sophie's choice between her children, improbable as that was, forced on Sophie by the equally improbable Dr. Jemand von Niemand. But Stingo is unable to restrain his impulse to stylistic embellishment. He taints the purity of Sophie's already melodramatic scream, "I can't choose! I can't choose!" with his private commentary that "Tormented angels never screamed so loudly above hell's pandemonium."[5] The compulsion to transform painful human moments into cosmic gestures through stylistic effects like this one makes the Holocaust a gratuitous literary event to be "written up" by an aspiring novelist like Stingo. This *separates* the history from the fiction by advertising the effort to absorb one into the other.

One other example should suffice to make this point. As Sophie's "battered memory" struggles for the last time to face the implications of her children's fate, Stingo again buries her efforts beneath the writer's mound of rhetoric: "She paused to look out through the night at the dark shore of the Virginia of our destination, removed by staggering dimensions of time and space from her own benighted, cursed, and—to me even at that moment—incomprehensible history" (495). One purpose of literary art, especially when confronting the Holocaust, is to encourage a perceiving consciousness to make comprehensible the incomprehensible, but Stingo's penchant for inflated style intervenes repeatedly at crucial potential moments of recognition like these, diverting the reader's attention from Sophie's trial to the writer's resolve to *render* it.

One might expect that Stingo, having extracted from Sophie her ultimate painful revelation, would have devoted himself to sympathy for the victim. But though Sophie's heart may have turned to stone, her body, to Stingo's delight, has retained its sumptuous sinuosity. Indeed, his failure as a perceiving consciousness is that he mistakes a climax for a denouement. On the page following Sophie's confession about her children's fate, Stingo's curiosity about her story is replaced by a night of erotic calisthenics that make one wonder where the focus of his interest has lain all along. What are we to make of this narrator, to say nothing of his narrative, which can literally juxtapose death in the gas chamber with lavish descriptions of the varieties of his sexual experience with Sophie? One longs to believe that here too Styron is indulging in parody; but once more, whether he is or not, the results are the same: to mock, to diminish, to negate the authenticity of Sophie's anguish in Auschwitz. Indeed, Stingo parodies Sophie and himself when he describes his last spasm of pleasure in Sophie's mouth in language reminiscent of her response to Dr. Jemand von Niemand's cruel challenge to her to choose between her children. Stingo says of himself: "I verged on a scream, or a prayer, and my vision went blank, and I gratefully perished" (498). So close to her Auschwitz narrative, such evocation of Sophie's language savors of the indecent. Her "oral testimony" itself has collapsed into a bizarre form of sexual parody, as speech disintegrates into suction.

In attempting to write a serious novel about the Holocaust using Stingo as narrator, Styron created for himself insuperable obstacles. Stingo's priapic sensibility, his obsession with tumescence, combined with his platitudinous anti-Semitic instincts, disqualify him for the literary task he chooses—to tell Sophie's story convincingly and sympathetically. The evidence is strewn throughout the narrative. Though Styron may have been indulging in some ethnic "humor" by having his narrator endlessly identify Jews with bagels, Manischewitz, and halvah, or longing to bury his nose in Leslie Lapidus's "damp Jewish bosom" (125), or feeling pleased with the clever turn of phrase that alludes to "window-shopping Hadassah matrons," or asking regretfully "Why, instead of the floundering, broke, unpublished writer that I was, couldn't I be an attractive, intelligent, well-paid Jewish urologist with a sexy wife?" (426)—whatever Styron's intentions, such tiresome facility for stereotyping eventually undermines Stingo's qualifications for the serious business of narrating and interpreting Sophie's Auschwitz background. And a parody of Sophie's ordeal would not be worth telling—certainly not worthy of Styron's talent as a writer. However Styron feels personally about these matters, his real choice of Stingo as perceiving consciousness proves fatal to our appreciation of Sophie's fictional choice in the novel. Stingo's failure betrays Styron's—and vice versa.

Saul Bellow will have none of the romantic sentimentalism that enables Stingo to speak of SS Doctor Jemand von Niemand as "a failed believer seeking redemption, groping for renewed faith" (485). Unlike Stingo, who magnifies the drama of Sophie's ordeal at every opportunity, Mr. Sammler is modest about what he has endured. It was not, he thinks, an achievement: "There was no special merit, there was no wizardry. There was only suffocation escaped" (273). The search for some intellectual, emotional, and spiritual "air" to liberate Sammler's consciousness from this stifling heritage constitutes the burden of the novel, and if his quest is not entirely successful, the fault is history's, not his. History, in the form of his Holocaust encounter with a mass grave, has estranged Sammler from his earlier enthusiasm for the utopian vision of H.G. Wells; it has also alienated him from the student generation of the sixties, which hoots him off the platform at Columbia, unaware of the genesis of his present condition of mind and hence totally unsympathetic to his position. Sammler is able to bring his Holocaust experience into the foreground of his *own* consciousness, and he does this throughout the novel; but he can bring it into no one else's, so must bear his memories and their consequences alone.

As a survivor, Sammler thinks near the end of the narrative, "he still has consciousness, earthliness, human actuality" (273). But instead of gaining him entrance to the community of men, these qualities isolate Sammler, since they issue from an exclusive background that he cannot share with others. Sammler consistently deflates the heroic and dramatic possibilities of his encounter with the pit, going so far as to suggest that only chance preserved his life: "If there had been another foot of dirt," he thinks. "Perhaps others *had* been buried alive in that ditch" (273). But this is not the stuff of romantic defiance and energy that the younger generation around Sammler thrives on; it offers a view diametrically opposed to the enthusiastic schemes of his daughter, his nephew, and his former son-in-law, schemes heedless of the ordeal Sammler has survived. *They* still dream of molding the future; Sammler has been shaped by his past.

And while he has not lapsed into the pessimism of his namesake, Arthur Schopenhauer, Mr. Sammler speaks of the "luxury of non-intimidation by doom" (134) as if he were fighting a rearguard action against the gloomy momentum of modern history. Between the pickpocket's phallic assertiveness against Sammler in the novel's opening episode (a sour if unintended commentary on Stingo's adolescent faith in the power of tumescence) and Eisen's gratuitous violence against the same culprit near the novel's end, Sammler gathers his musings and meditations to find some small justification for his belief that the earth might still be, as he calls it, a "glorious planet" (135). This is in spite of his simultaneous perception that everything was being done by its inhabitants "to make it intolerable to abide here, an unconscious collaboration of all souls spreading madness and poison" (135). Because he himself has had to kill in order to survive, because he has had impressed on him not only the idea but also the experience of life as a mausoleum, Sammler develops internal resistance to the threat of becoming a "bad joke of the self," a threat that both Sophie and Stingo (and Styron?) succumb to when they allow sexual acrobatics to displace sober confrontation with the possibility of the universe as mausoleum. Bellow excludes from his vision the incongruity, not to say the inconsistency of character, that Styron incorporates, thus acknowledging a continuity between Holocaust past and post-Holocaust present that Stingo seems immune to. From the "harsh surgery" of immersion in mass dying, Sammler reflects, one "cannot come out intact" (230). "I assume I am one of you," he volunteers to his audience, "But also I am not" (230). This dual vision constitutes the essence of his perception, what we might call his "good eye" and "bad eye" seeing, the fusion of background and foreground that characterizes his peculiar point of view.

In the end, the main difference between Stingo and Sammler is that Stingo is unable to avoid experiencing Sophie's encounter with atrocity as a writer rather than as a fellow human being. Sammler, on the other hand, has endured the Holocaust in all his creatureliness; his human actuality, as he thinks, is a blend of earthliness and consciousness. Stingo reserves his own encounter with the symbolic grave for the closing paragraphs of *Sophie's Choice*, but his allusion gives away the literary inspiration that has been guiding his investigation from the beginning. Falling asleep on the beach at Coney Island, he tells us, he had "abominable dreams—which seemed to be a compendium of all the tales of Edgar Allan Poe" (515). One would think that Sophie's experience might be enough to shape his nightmares. He views reality through his literary heritage: "All night long I had the sensation of helplessness, speechlessness, an inability to move or cry out against the inexorable weight of the earth as it was flung in *thud-thud-thud*ing rhythm against my rigidly paralyzed, supine body, a living cadaver being prepared for burial in the sands of Egypt" (515).

What Styron has given us in Stingo is the immense, overwhelming egoism of the literary imagination. Sammler condenses into two words—"suffocation escaped"—the ponderous distance between living cadavers in the landscape of Poe and his own escape from "the sand clay and stones of Poland" (273). Stingo's last legacy, to no one's surprise, is some lines from a poem, acknowledging his dream of death but affirming nonetheless *"in glory, the bright, the morning star"* (515). The novel's last words, "excellent and fair," are also from a poem—this time by Emily Dickinson. Are we to assume that literary vision so easily displaces Holocaust fact in the foreground of our imagination?

Once again, Mr. Sammler's concluding aspirations are more modest. The scene of his life has shifted from a mass grave and a mausoleum to a morgue, where the body of his friend Elya Gruner lies in the repose of death. For Sammler, life has become a post-mortem on the implications of his survival; so perhaps it is fitting that his last reflections should be on the fate that links all human beings—the corpse Elya Gruner mirrors our common destiny. Sammler's last gesture of tribute and commemoration is not literary, but human, humbling rather than assertive, even self-effacing: it is the legacy of an aging man, even as the Holocaust is the legacy of an aging planet. What Sammler "knows" in the novel's closing words is, as he had thought earlier, "To be so powerless was death" (289). He does indeed see himself as a *"past* person," someone "between the human and the non-human states, between content and emptiness, between full and void, meaning and not-meaning, between this world and no world" (290). He meditates on the limits within which life on the post-Holocaust planet fluctuates, a shrinking area where Mr. Sammler's melancholy memories leave some space for the decently human and the humanly decent. Holocaust fact and literary fiction share the constraints of these limits. The novels of Bellow and Styron reflect the difficulty of maintaining an equilibrium between them.

NOTES

1. Norma Rosen, "The Second Life of Holocaust Imagery." *Witness,* Spring 1987, vol. 1, no. 1, p. 14.

2. A. Anatoli (Kuznetsov), *Babi Yar: A Document in the Form of a Novel,* trans. David Floyd. New York: Farrar, Straus and Giroux, 1970, p. 98.

3. D.M. Thomas, *The White Hotel.* New York: Pocket Books, 1981, p. 287.

4. Saul Bellow, *Mr. Sammler's Planet.* New York: Viking Press, 1970, pp. 289–290. Subsequent references will be included in the text.

5. William Styron, *Sophie's Choice.* New York: Random House, 1979, p. 483. Subsequent references will be included in the text.

Holocaust and Autobiography: Wiesel, Friedländer, Pisar

Joseph Sungolowsky

Autobiography is usually defined as a retrospective narrative written about one's life, in the first person and in prose. Such writing has appeared with increasing frequency in Western literature since the beginning of the nineteenth century. As a result of the events of World War II, it gained considerable significance in France, as can be seen in the works of authors such as André Malraux and Simone de Beauvoir. In view of the proliferation of autobiography, the recent studies by the critics Philippe Lejeune and Georges May have attempted to examine its characteristics and determine to what extent it could represent a literary genre.

The history of the destruction of European Jewry by the Nazis has relied heavily upon the accounts written by survivors, which will probably remain a prime source of information concerning the magnitude of the catastrophe. Autobiography written as a result of experiences lived during the Holocaust is therefore an integral part of its literature. Since such literature cannot be linked to any of the norms of literary art, it has been termed a literature of "atrocity" or "decomposition." Holocaust autobiography inherits, therefore, the problematic aspect of both autobiography and the literature of the Holocaust. In the light of the above-mentioned studies on autobiography and on the basis of *Night* (1958) by Elie Wiesel, *When Memory Comes* (1978) by Saul Friedländer, and *Of Blood and Hope* (1979) and *La Ressource humaine* (1983) by Samuel Pisar, we shall examine who writes Holocaust autobiography, why and how it is written, and what is the substance of such writing.

I

Autobiography is generally written in midlife by an author who has achieved fame thanks to previous works which have been rec-

ognized for their value, or by an individual who has played a significant
role in public life. Saul Friedländer was 46 years old when *When
Memory Comes* was published. At that time, he had gained an
international reputation as a historian of Nazism. Samuel Pisar was
50 when he wrote *Of Blood and Hope.* He is also the author of
Coexistence and Commerce (1970), an impressive political and economic
treatise advocating trade relations between East and West, especially
as a means to ease the Cold War. He, too, has achieved recognition
as a political scientist, as an advisor to governments, and as an
international lawyer.

Writing autobiography at an earlier age or as a first book is
considered an exception.[1] Elie Wiesel's *Night* is such an exception.
He recounts how fortuitous his career as a writer was in its beginnings,
especially considering that he might not have survived the concentration camps at all. Upon his liberation, he vowed not to speak of
his experience for at least ten years. It was the French novelist François
Mauriac who persuaded him to tell his story, and Wiesel adds that
at the time Mauriac was as well-known as he was obscure.[2] Thus,
at the age of 28, Wiesel published his autobiographical narrative
concerning his experience in the concentration camps, first in Yiddish
under the title *Un die velt hot geshvigen,* subsequently in French under
the title *La Nuit.* In 1976, Wiesel stated that *Night* could have remained
his one and only book;[3] indeed, when he began to write fiction, the
French critic René Lalou wondered how Wiesel could have undertaken
to write anything else after *Night.*[4] Clearly, at the time Wiesel published
Night, he lacked the fame as an author of previous works usually
expected of an autobiography, as indicated by Philippe Lejeune and
Georges May.[5]

An autobiography is deemed authentic when there is identity
between the name of the author appearing on the title page and the
narrator of the story.[6] In *Night,* Wiesel relates that during a rollcall
in Auschwitz, he heard a man crying out: "Who among you is Wiesel
from Sighet?" He turned out to be relative that had been deported
from Antwerp. Subsequently, Wiesel is called by his first name "Eliezer"
by that relative, by Juliek, a fellow-inmate, and by his father.[7] Friedländer refers to his name several times in the course of his narrative.
He recalls how difficult it was for him to get accustomed to his new
first-name "Paul-Henri" given to him in the Catholic boarding school
in France, as he was called "Pavel" or "Pawlicek," the diminutive
given to him by his family. He names himself again when he recalls
his stay, in 1950, with an uncle who directed an institution for mentally
ill children. One of them tried to communicate with him during a
fit, and all he could say was "Herr Friedländer." (Friedländer sees

in this incident an example of the unlocking of the inner world which he experienced himself when he began to write his book.)

Pisar names himself throughout *Of Blood and Hope*. Upon returning to Auschwitz as a member of a delegation to a commemorative ceremony, he describes himself as follows: "a reincarnated Samuel Pisar clothed simply in his respectable attire of international lawyer, scholar, American citizen had to step into the light and avow once more that once, not so long ago, he had crawled in the pain, the filth and the degradation of the factories of death."[8] Later on, he quotes Solzhenitsyn commenting upon his views on coexistence between East and West: "Pisar is one of the few to see clearly."[9]

Autobiography is considered genuine when the author states, either in the text itself or in connection with it, that his intent has indeed been autobiographical. Lejeune calls such a statement an "autobiographical pact"—an agreement between author and reader according to which the reader is assured that he is reading the truth.[10]

Upon the publication of his book, Friedländer told an interviewer that he wrote it as a result of an "inner necessity," and he discussed its main themes: his childhood, his life as a youngster in a Catholic boarding school after he was separated from his parents during the war, his discovery of Zionism and his views on Israel where he lives.[11] In the preface to the French edition of his book, Pisar explains that in order to write it he had to revive from within the depths of his self the tragic episodes of his life which represent such a sharp contrast with his "reincarnation" as a brilliant public figure.[12] Pisar's subsequent book intitled *La Ressource humaine* is of a similar intent. It opens as follows: "I sleep with eyes half-closed. I have done so for the last forty years. Even since I entered the precincts of Auschwitz."[13] Wiesel's autobiographical pact was established twenty years after the publication of *Night*, when he told an interviewer: "*Night*, my first narrative, was an autobiographical story, a kind of testimony of one witness speaking of his own life, his own death."[14]

II

Autobiography is written in order to come to terms with oneself.[15] Recapturing the past is, therefore, the most common preoccupation of the autobiographer. This motivation is repeatedly stressed by Saul Friedländer whose childhood was shattered by the events of the war. Recounting his suicide attempt after he was separated from his parents, he wonders whether he is the same person or even the same Jew "if there were such a thing as a collective Jew."[16] When he tries to seek out a former schoolmate 35 years later, he suspects that this impulse

LIBRARY ST. MARY'S COLLEGE

is dictated by the "need for synthesis . . . that no longer excludes anything."[17] Therefore, in order to recapture the past, his sole recourse is to write, for "writing retraces the contours of the past. . . , it does at least preserve a presence."[18] In measuring the distance between past and present, Friedländer realizes that he has retained a reticence toward people, a tendency to passivity, moral preoccupations and self-examination inculcated to him by the "taboos" of his former Catholic education.[19]

In searching for himself, the autobiographer may indulge in narcissism and conceit.[20] Pisar hardly avoids these temptations. Self-glorification is a pervasive theme in both of his autobiographical books. He dwells extensively upon his close relationships with world celebrities, on his brilliance as a political scientist whose advice is sought by statesmen, on his participation in international conferences where he is eagerly listened to, on his talent at handling the affairs of renowned movie stars. However, such vanity seems deliberate, for Pisar never fails to stress the contrast between his present success and his former condition as a concentration camp inmate. He often recalls "the young boy with a shaven head, pale skin tightly drawn over his face, and an almost broken body."[21] In *La Ressource humaine,* he writes: "I carry the immense privilege of a double experience. That of a sub-human thrown in the deepest hell of the century and that of an individual treasured by the great and productive cultures of this planet that are still free."[22]

Autobiography is written as a testimony, especially when the author has lived a particular moment of history that must not be forgotten.[23] Such was Elie Wiesel's intent when he wrote *Night.* For him, "Auschwitz was a unique phenomenon, a unique event, like the revelation at Sinai."[24] Had it not been for the war, he would not have become a storyteller but would have written on philosophy, the Bible, and the Talmud. He recalls that as he looked at himself in the mirror after his liberation, he realized how much he had changed and decided that someone had to write about that change. Although he had vowed to remain silent for ten years, he had absorbed "the obsession to tell the tale." He states: "I knew that anyone who remained alive had to become a story-teller, a messenger, had to speak up."[25]

Autobiography may also be written to educate. The autobiographer wishes his reader to learn from his experience.[26] In the preface to the French edition of *Blood and Hope,* Pisar writes that he did not mean to write a narrative describing the atrocities of the Holocaust or an abstract ideological work on the subject, but: "to forget those four hellish years spent in the most loathsome trashcan of history."[27] For him, the danger of a thermonuclear war is a mere repetition of the former madness. He writes, therefore, to educate the youth of today. "They need to arm themselves against the tragedies, the hypocrisies, the false gods of history."[28] In *La Ressource humaine*, Pisar further explores the means by which a third world war can be avoided. The autobiographical element is present in it again, and with the same educational intent. He relates that while he was about to enter the gas chamber, he escaped from the line, seized a brush and pail, and began scrubbing the floor of the waiting room much to the liking of the guards. He is convinced, therefore, that the world possesses likewise the resources to avoid a nuclear war.[29]

III

No matter how sincere or truthful the autobiographer intends to be, he must face the technical and literary problems related to the writing. Such problems are even more acute in the case of Holocaust autobiography. Before they write autobiography, authors will make sure that a reasonable amount of time has elapsed between the events they wish to relate and the actual writing. Such "distanciation" ensures orderliness to the narrative. In the case of Holocaust autobiography, the waiting period is not only technical but also emotional. Elie Wiesel states that he feared being unable to live up to the past, "of saying the wrong things, of saying too much or too little." He therefore decided to wait ten years before writing.[30] Friedländer stated that he had unsuccessfully attempted to write his account fifteen years earlier.[31] Pisar waited about 35 years before he decided to write.

With the best faith or memory in the world, it is impossible to re-create in writing a reality long gone by.[32] In this respect, Holocaust autobiographers are even more frustrated. They constantly suspect that whatever the form and content of their narrative, they have not succeeded in conveying the past adequately. Wiesel feels that, while *Night* is the center of his work, "what happened during that night . . . will not be revealed."[33] In the midst of writing, Friedländer feels "deeply discouraged." He writes: "I will never be able to express what I want to say; these lines, often clumsy, are very far removed, I know, from my memories, and even my memories retrieve only sparse fragments of my parents' existence, of their world, of the time when I was a child." At the conclusion of his book, he is still wondering whether he has succeeded "in setting down even so much as a tiny part of what [he] wanted to express."[34] However, since they represent an attempt to recapture whatever is retained of the past, such memories, as fragmented as they may be, remain invaluable. As put by Leon Wieseltier, they are "all the more illuminating, because memory is the consciousness of things and events that have not yet disappeared completely into knowledge."[35]

No matter how truthful the autobiographer tries to be, he cannot avoid having recourse to fictional or literary devices. Indeed, autobiography is necessarily linked to related literary genres such as the novel, the theater, the diary, or the chronicle.[36] Thus, despite Theodore W. Adorno's contention that it is barbaric to write literature after Auschwitz, the Holocaust writer or autobiographer must engage in a "writing experience" if he wishes to express himself.

The terse language of Wiesel's *Night* is occasionally broken by harrowing scenes such as that of Madame Shachter gone mad in the cattle car or by dialogues such as those that take place between himself and his erstwhile master Moshe-the-Beadle or with his dying father. Fantasy is present when he depicts his native Sighet as "an open tomb" after its Jews have been rounded up. He uses irony when he recalls that a fellow inmate has faith in Hitler because he has kept all his promises to the Jewish people. Images express the author's feelings. Gallows set up in the assembly place in preparation of a hanging appear to him as "three black crows," and the violin of a fellow inmate who has died after playing a Beethoven concerto lies beside him like "a strange overwhelming little corpse." The grotesque best portrays his fellow inmates, "Poor mountebanks, wider than they were tall, more dead than alive; poor clowns, their ghostlike faces emerging from piles of prison clothes! Buffoons!"[37]

While Friedländer and Pisar are not writers in the artistic sense of the word, they cannot avoid resorting to literary devices. On page 78 of *When Memory Comes*, Friedländer writes in a footnote: "All the names associated with my stay in Montluçon, the Indre and Sweden are fictitious," clearly a technique widely used by discretion-conscious autobiographers and by authors of autobiographical novels.[38] The universe of the concentration camp has imprinted on Pisar's mind indelible images and myths. Upon visiting the naval base at Norfolk, Virginia, he is impressed by the latest inventions in warfare such as the nuclear aircraft carriers. The white star which adorns one of them reminds him of the same emblem on the American tank that liberated him. Witnessing the array of these formidable weapons meant to be used in a third world war, he cannot help but seeing in them a "nuclear gas chamber."[39]

According to Georges May, reproducing letters and evoking historical episodes enliven autobiography and enhance its authenticity.[40] Friedländer reproduces correspondence related to his childhood in France. There are letters written by his mother to the guardian to whose care she entrusted him, by his father to the director of the Catholic school authorizing her to baptize the child; and he reproduces the last letter written by both parents from the train that took them to the death camp. There are letters written by himself after the Liberation to his new guardians inquiring about the fate of his parents and eventually informing them that he would not return home since he had decided to leave for the newly born State of Israel. Retracing the stages of his ascent from a subhuman survivor to his present position, Pisar rarely misses an opportunity to name the celebrities with whom he associated. As a student in Australia, he took walks with Prime Minister Menzies. At Harvard, Ralph Nader and Zaki Yamani were his classmates. During a ceremony in Auschwitz, he stood next to Giscard d'Estaing of France and Gierek of Poland. At the World Gathering of Holocaust Survivors, he stood next to Begin. *Of Blood and Hope* includes a centerfold where he is pictured with Kissinger, Arthur Rubinstein, etc. Mitterand agrees with his views on coexistence between East and West. He is the lawyer of Richard Burton, Ava Gardner, and Catherine Deneuve.

IV

While autobiography may choose to embrace a greater or smaller part of one's life, Holocaust autobiography will essentially deal with the period marked by the events of the Nazi genocide. Just as any autobiography related to a troubled historical period acquires an added significance,[41] so does Holocaust autobiography exert a unique fascination upon the reader because of its central motive.

Like many autobiographers who try to resurrect their happy past, Wiesel, Pisar, and Friedländer dwell upon their childhood as they recall their native towns, their families, and their early schooling shortly before the outbreak of the war. Wiesel and Pisar are sons of educated fathers who were actively involved in Jewish communal affairs. While Friedländer's father had not retained much from his early Jewish education, he was not indifferent to his origins. At the age of 12, Wiesel was eager to study the Kabbalah with his enigmatic teacher Moshe-the-Beadle in his native Sighet. Pisar's native city, Bialystok, is a "vibrant center of Jewish cultural life," where socialism and Zionism mingle and vie with the study of Torah. As he studies for his Bar Mitzvah, which takes place in the ghetto, he realizes that the persecutions which beset the Jewish people throughout its history had forged its very identity. For Friedländer the child, his native Prague is a city of legends, especially that of the Golem, the robot built by the sixteenth-century Rabbi Loewe to protect the endangered Jews of the city. While attending the English school in that city,

Friedländer becomes aware of his Jewishness as he is invited to leave catechism classes and told to attend instead Jewish religious instruction.

These evocations of childhood are all the more dramatic as they abrutply came to an end. As he completes the recollection of his early childhood, Friedländer writes: "I hesitate somehow to leave this calm and, when all is said and done, happy period of my life."[42] What follows in the writings of all three authors are scenes of departures. When Wiesel's family must join the roundup of Jews in Sighet, he sees his father weeping for the first time. Looking at his little sister, Tzipora, he notices that "the bundle on her back was too heavy for her."[43] On the eve of the family's departure from Prague, Friedländer is ceremoniously given a ring by his father so that he may not forget his native city. What is concealed from him is that they are fleeing the Nazis. Before leaving the house for the ghetto of Bialystok, Pisar's father gathers his family in the drawing-room, lights a big fire in the fireplace, throws in it the most cherished mementoes of the family and states: "We are living our last moments in our home. We don't know when we will return. We don't know who will move in here after we are gone."[44]

As painful as it may be to both author and reader, these autobiographical writings attempt to come to grips with the hard reality of the concentrationary universe. If *Night* has become a classic, it is because it remains one of the most concise and factual eyewitness accounts of the horrors. Wiesel goes into such details as the early disbelief of the victims ("The yellow star? Oh! well, what of it?" says his own father), the anguish of those who have been marked by death by Mengele in the course of a selection and Wiesel's own joy at having escaped it, the careless trampling of inmates by their own comrades in the course of the agonizing death marches.

The opening pages of Pisar's *Of Blood and Hope* are dedicated to a rather detailed account of his life in the concentration camps. Among the numerous descriptions of his experiences is a shattering portrait of a dying inmate, called "Musulman" in concentration camp terminology. Such an individual who had succeeded in escaping many a selection, once given that label by his own fellow-inmates, "was left feeling he had exhausted his last reserves of strength and hope," and would drop lifeless while no one cared.[45] However, most of his experiences as a former inmate are related in the light of his activities as a political or economic advisor. When he addresses a session of the Bundestag in Bonn, he finds irony in the fact that his previous dialogue with the Germans was a one sided: "caps off, caps on!" coming from his guards.[46] He feels that it is utterly dangerous to subject economy to a nondemocratic regime. Under Nazism, such an alliance led to the I. G. Farben phenomenon which treated human beings as "an expandable raw material . . . from which all vital force was first extracted, was then treated with Zyklon B gas so that it could yield its secondary products: gold teeth and fillings for the Reichsbank, hair for the mattresses, grease for the soap and skin for the lampshades."[47] The struggle for inalienable human rights must go on. In the concentration camps, many died with the conviction that no one would ever learn of their utter suffering, while today violations of human rights anywhere are swiftly publicized to the world at large.[48]

Unlike Wiesel and Pisar, Friedländer did not experience concentration-camp life. Yet, the Holocaust remains a central theme of his book. He relates how he narrowly escaped a transport of children rounded up by the French police as a result of an agreement between the Vichy government and the Nazis. As for other typical aspects of the Holocaust, one might say that he attempts to live them vicariously. As an adult, he visits the village on the French-Swiss border where his parents were kept from crossing into Switzerland, handed over to the French police, and returned to a concentration camp in France while awaiting deportation. Upon the anniversary of the Warsaw ghetto uprising, he meditates about a story told by a survivor concerning a boy begging for a piece of bread in the ghetto and dying before he could reach the piece thrown to him by the narrator from his window. Eight years before the release of *Shoah*, the film by Claude Lanzman, Friedländer relates the detailed testimony concerning the destruction of the Jews at Treblinka given by a former SS guard to Lanzman.[49] He writes that he must leave the room when he hears a former SS officer telling about the burning of villages in Russia where he served. He is appalled when Admiral Dönitz, Hitler's successor, tells him that he knew nothing of the extermination of the Jews, and when he does research in Germany, he feels the urge to pack up and leave. Yet, Friedländer admits that he is unable to fathom the reality of Belzec and Maidanek. He writes: "The veil between the events and me had not been rent. I had lived on the edges of the catastrophe . . . and despite all my efforts, I remained in my own eyes not so much a victim as a spectator."[50]

V

"Autobiography," writes Georges May, "is capable of absorbing the most diverse material, to assimilate it and to change it into autobiography."[51] Inasmuch as Holocaust autobiography deals with the events of one of the greatest upheavals of the twentieth century and the most traumatic destruction of the Jewish people, it is natural that autobiographers reflect upon the impact of those events on their personality, on the destiny of the Jewish people and on the post-Holocaust world.

Confession is an essential ingredient of autobiography. Its degree of sincerity remains the sole prerogative of the autobiographer who can choose to shield himself behind his own writing. In Wiesel's *Night*, the frankness of his confession serves as a testimony to the extent of the dehumanization he has reached as a result of his concentration-camp life. While he has been separated forever from his mother and sister upon arrival in Auschwitz, he has managed to stay with his father. Both have miraculously escaped selection for death on several occasions. Yet, the survival instinct has overtaken him in the face of his dying father. When a guard tells him that in the camp "there are no fathers, no brothers, no friends," he thinks in his innermost heart that the guard is right but does not dare admit it. When he wakes up the next morning (less than four months before the Liberation) to find his father dead, he thinks "something like— free at last."[52] Henceforth, Wiesel's life is devoid of meaning. *Night* concludes with the episode of the author looking at himself in the mirror. He writes: "a corpse gazed at me. The look in his eyes as they stared into mine has never left me."[53] As indicated by Ellen Fine, the shift from the first to the third person in that sentence points to the "fragmented self,"[54] and, as indicated by Wiesel himself, that sight was to determine his career as a "writer-witness."[55]

Friedländer informs us of the psychological effects the separation from his parents has had on his childhood. An immediate result of it is his attempted suicide followed by nightmarish fits of fever during which he is vainly looking for his mother in rolling trains. "Passing by the hospital where his father lay sick, he wonders, "if one of the glass doors wouldn't suddenly open and [my] mother or father lean out over the edge of the terrace to signal discreetly to [me]."[56] Without news from his parents, he becomes very devout, worshipping especially the Virgin Mary for he rediscovered in her "something of the presence of a mother."[57] When he does not see his parents return after the Liberation, anxiety overtakes him, and he describes in detail its physiological and psychological effects."[58] To this day, the adult remains unsettled by his past. He writes: "In my heart of hearts, I still feel a strange attraction, mingled with profound repulsion, for this phase of my childhood."[59]

The Holocaust causes all three writers to question God's ways. One of the main themes of *Night* is Wiesel's shattered faith. When he recalls his arrival in Auschwitz, he writes the now famous words:

"Never shall I forget those flames which consumed my faith forever."[60] He subsequently doubts God's justice,[61] argues with God on Rosh-Hashanah,[62] eats on Yom Kippur as an act of defiance against God, and feels that God Himself is hanging on the gallows when he witnesses the hanging of a child.[63] In fact, the "Trial of God"[64] obsesses Wiesel throughout his work. Without being specifically preoccupied with metaphysics in their account, both Friedländer and Pisar seem nevertheless to take God to task. In the last letter written to his guardian, Friedländer's parents express the wish that God may repay and bless her, which prompts the author's comment: "What God was meant?"[65] Upon being separated forever from his mother and sister, Pisar, too, raises his fist to heaven "in a blasphemous cry towards the Almighty."[66]

Many inmates were able to survive by means of "spiritual resistance"—by clinging to an ideal which would keep them from being destroyed against all odds. For Pisar, such an ideal was friendship in the camps with Ben, a childhood friend, and with Nico, "a resourceful older ally in the daily struggle against death."[67] Having escaped death on several occasions, it is they that he seeks out and it is with them that he is ultimately reunited until they were liberated. For Pisar, this lasting friendship not only meant that they had endured the Holocaust together but also proved that "man can overcome, if he has the courage not to despair."[68]

Having reasonably distanced themselves from the events of the Holocaust before they engaged into autobiographical writing, Friedländer and Pisar are able to put their experience in perspective and, therefore, reflect upon Jewish destiny and identity and express views on the post-Holocaust world.

If, as a child, Friedländer is fascinated by the legend of the Golem or by the sacrifice of Isaac, to the adult, the former symbolizes Jewish "perpetual restlessness"[69] and the latter Jewish obedience to "some mysterious destiny."[70] Upon discovering Zionism after the war, he becomes convinced that a state is needed so that the Jewish people may never again go to the slaughter like sheep.[71] Recalling that his father had waited to become a refugee in France to tell him the Hannukah story, he realizes that his father had rediscovered a "permanent and lasting" feeling of kinship to the community only as a result of the crisis.[73] He himself observes sincere Jewish prayer while living with a religious guardian after the war,[74] experiences a genuine feeling of Jewishness upon discovering Hasidism in the books of Martin Buber,[75] and, on the occasion of Yom Kippur 1977, he states that one can hardly define the Jewish people without the Jewish religion.[76] As an Israeli, Friedländer would like to see his country at peace. He wonders, therefore, whether Israel fails "to accept compromise at the proper moment."[77] He acknowledges, however, that the Jewish people has always been engaged in an "endless quest" which is symbolic of that pursued by mankind as a whole.[78] Therefore, Friedländer surmises that Israel is not likely to alter the course of Jewish history.[79]

Pisar views Jewish destiny and the post-Holocaust world solely with the eyes of a survivor. He concludes the account of a family trip to Masada, the historic symbol of Jewish resistance, with the words "No more Auschwitz, no more Masada."[80] The existence of the State of Israel and the freedom of Soviet Jews are causes that are very close to his heart. The sight of Israeli soldiers praying at the Wailing Wall they had just conquered during the Six-Day War convinces him that "the trains headed for Treblinka, Maidanek and Auschwitz had finally reached their destination."[81] He is indignant at the UN resolution which equates Zionism with racism. It causes him to question his own survival and to realize that perhaps "there was no way to escape from the mentality of the ghettos and the camps after all."[82] Therefore, Israel must remain the ultimate "haven for survivors," especially in the light of recent attacks upon Jews in Europe, which show that the Jew remains prime target.[83] He is heartened by the fact that a Jewish community continues to exist in the Soviet Union sixty five years after the revolution. As a member of an American delegation to a conference on *détente* that took place in Kiev in 1971, he daringly confronts the Russians with their persistant anti-Semitic policy. Introducing himself as a survivor, he criticizes them for requiring that the word JEW be inscribed on the identity cards of Soviet Jews and for failing to recognize Babi Yar as the burial place of thousands of Jews killed by the Nazis.[84] Nevertheless, Pisar remains unequivocally committed to the idea of peaceful coexistence, which is the underlying idea of his autobiographical writings. When he is reminded that, as a survivor, he ought to advocate a militant attitude toward the Russians, he replies that firmness and open mindedness in dealing with them are not incompatible.[85]

Meant as a stark narrative of the events and despite the ten-year period that preceded its writing, Wiesel's *Night* is devoid of reflections extraneous to his experiences in the concentration camps. He has stated that, except for *Night*, his other works are not autobiographical, although he occasionally brings into them "autobiographical data and moods."[86] Yet, Wiesel has emphasized the importance of *Night* as the foundation of his subsequent works. He states: "*Night*, my first narrative, was an autobiographical story, a kind of testimony of one witness speaking of his own life, his own death. All kinds of options were available: suicide, madness, killing, political action, hate, friend-ship. I note all these options: faith, rejection of faith, blasphemy, atheism, denial, rejection of man, despair, and in each book I explore one aspect. In *Dawn*, I explore the political action; in *The Accident*, suicide; in *The Town Beyond the Wall*, madness; in *The Gates of the Forest*, faith and friendship; in *A Beggar in Jerusalem*, history, the return. All the stories are one story except that I build them in concentric circles. The center is the same and is in *Night*."[87] Such a position illustrates Philippe Lejeune's concept of "autobiographical space."[88] Indeed, according to Lejeune, it is not always possible to derive the total image of a writer solely on the basis of a work explicitly declared to be autobiographical. Such an image is to be sought rather in the totality of his work which cannot fail to contain autobiographical data. Reflections on Jewish destiny and identity and on the post-Holocaust world are surely the very essence of Wiesel's writings whether they take the form of fiction, tales, plays, or essays.

*   *   *

Autobiography does not necessarily encompass a whole life. Many autobiographers choose to write about a part of it which they deem significant enough to reflect a profound if not crucial human experience. The Holocaust illustrates this aspect of autobiographical writing. As recognized authors in their respective fields, Wiesel, Friedländer, and Pisar feel a compelling need at one point or another in their lives to tell of their experiences. Whether they write to settle the past, to testify or to educate, they mobilize a variety of devices and themes available to the autobiographer who seeks to share his experiences with the reader. As the Holocaust continues to be represented in an ever-growing multiplicity of forms, autobiography remains a fascinating means to express it. It is noteworthy, therefore, that the Holocaust autobiographer encounters consciously or not many of the problems faced by any autobiographer. However, in the case of the Holocaust autobiographer, such problems become even more crucial because of the nature of the material he is dealing with. Autobiography uni-versalizes one's life. In the hands of the writers examined in this study, Holocaust autobiography not only serves as an invaluable testimony of events that must never be forgotten, but also strengthens the feeling of all those who wish to identify with the victims of the greatest crime that ever took place amidst modern civilization.

NOTES

1. Georges May, *L'Autobiographie*. Paris: Presses Universitaires de France, 1979, pp. 33–39.

2. Elie Wiesel, *A Jew Today*. New York: Random House, 1978, pp. 14–19.

3. *Harry James Cargas in Conversation with Elie Wiesel*. New York: Paulist Press, 1976, p. 88.

4. Quoted by Wladimir Rabi, "Elie Wiesel: Un homme, une oeuvre, un public." *Esprit*, Sept. 1980, p. 81.

5. Philippe Lejeune, *Le Pacte autobiographique*. Paris: Editions du Seuil, 1975, p. 23; May, pp. 31–32.

6. Lejeune, p. 26.

7. I disagree with Ted L. Estess who sees a discrepancy between "Eliezer" the story-teller and "Elie" the author, which he interprets as a device of "distanciation" between the character and the author who is unable to fully retell the horror he has witnessed. See Ted L. Estess, *Elie Wiesel*, New York: Ungar, 1980, pp. 17–18. One should bear in mind that the original edition in Yiddish carries the first name "Eliezer" on its title page. Furthermore, Wiesel has unequivocally stressed the symbolic importance of his full Hebrew name "Eliezer ben Chlomo." See Cargas, p. 52.

8. Samuel Pisar, *Of Blood and Hope*. Boston, Toronto: Little, Brown & Co., 1979, p. 18.

9. *Ibid.*, p. 64.

10. Philippe Lejeune, *L'Autobiographie en France*. Paris: Armand Colin, 1971, p. 23.

11. Jacques Sabbath, "Israël à coeur ouvert," *L'Arche*, Nov. 1978, p. 35.

12. Samuel Pisar, *Le Sang et l'espoir*, Paris: Laffont, 1979, pp. 12–13. (Translations from that work are my own.)

13. Samuel Pisar, *La Ressource humaine*. Paris: Jean-Claude Lattès, 1983, p. 15. (Translations from that work are my own.)

14. Cargas, p. 86.

15. Lejeune, *L'Autobiographie*, p. 19; May, p. 55.

16. Saul Friedländer, *When Memory Comes*. New York: Avon Books, 1980, p. 100.

17. *Ibid.*, p. 114.

18. *Ibid.*, p. 135.

19. *Ibid.*, p. 164.

20. May, p. 160.

21. Pisar, *Of Blood and Hope*, p. 188.

22. Pisar, *La Ressource humaine*, p. 351.

23. May, p. 43.

24. Cargas, p. 8.

25. *Ibid.*, p. 87.

26. Lejeune, *L'Autobiographie*, p. 82.

27. Pisar, *Le Sang et l'espoir*, p. 20.

28. Pisar, *Of Blood and Hope*, p. 23.

29. Pisar, *La Ressource humaine*, pp. 47–49.

30. Cargas, p. 87.

31. Sabbath, p. 35.

32. May, p. 82.

33. Cargas, p. 86.

34. Friedländer, pp. 134, 182.

35. "Between Paris and Jerusalem," *New York Review of Books*, Oct. 25, 1979, p. 3.

36. Lejeune, *L'Autobiographie*, p. 28; May, pp. 113–116.

37. Elie Wiesel, *Night*. New York: Avon Books, 1969, p. 94. For a literary evaluation of *Night*, see Lawrence L. Langer, *The Holocaust and the Literary Imagination*. New Haven & London: Yale University Press, 1975, pp. 75–89; Ted L. Estess, *Elie Wiesel*, pp. 17–32.

38. Lejeune, *L'Autobiographie*, p. 83; May, p. 194.

39. Pisar, *La Ressource humaine*, pp. 216–217.

40. May, pp. 133–135.

41. *Ibid.*, p. 103.

42. Friedländer, p. 15.

43. Wiesel, *Night*, p. 29.

44. Pisar, *Of Blood and Hope*, p. 35.

45. *Ibid.*, p. 75.

46. *Ibid.*, p. 230.

47. *Ibid.*, p. 248.

48. Pisar, *La Ressource humaine*, p. 333.

49. Friedländer, pp. 116–117. See the testimony of Franz Suchomel in Claude Lanzman, *Shoah*. New York: Pantheon Books, 1985. In a letter to this writer, Saul Friedländer has confirmed his reporting of this testimony prior to the release of the film.

50. Friedländer, p. 155.

51. May, pp. 200–201.

52. Wiesel, *Night*, pp. 122–124. For a thorough and moving analysis of the father-son relationship in *Night*, See Ellen S. Fine, *Legacy of Night: The Literary Universe of Elie Wiesel*. Albany: State University Press, 1982, pp. 18–26.

53. Wiesel, *Night*, p. 127.

54. Fine, p. 25.

55. Cargas, p. 88.

56. Friedländer, p. 118.

57. *Ibid.*, p. 122.

58. *Ibid.*, pp. 132–133.

59. *Ibid.*, p. 140.

60. Wiesel, *Night*, p. 44.

61. *Ibid.*, p. 55.

62. *Ibid.*, p. 79.

63. *Ibid.*, p. 76.

64. Such is indeed the title of one of Wiesel's plays.

65. Friedländer, p. 90.

66. Pisar, *Of Blood and Hope*, p. 43.

67. *Ibid.*, p. 69.

68. *Ibid.*, p. 297.

69. Friedländer, p. 19.

70. *Ibid.*, p. 29.

71. *Ibid.*, p. 161.

72. *Ibid.*, p. 96.

73. *Ibid.*, p. 69.

74. *Ibid.*, p. 149.

75. *Ibid.*, pp. 103–104.

76. *Ibid.*, p. 123.

77. *Ibid.*, p. 182–183.

78. *Ibid.*, p. 83.

79. Leon Wieseltier's review of *When Memory Comes* (above, note 35) ascribes to the work political overtones which seem exaggerated to this writer.

80. Pisar, *Le Sang et l'espoir,* p. 303.

81. Pisar, of *Blood and Hope,* p. 54. Wiesel also writes on the same occasion: "Thus, by inviting hallucination and then rejecting it, I plunge into it and find friends, parents and neighbors, all the dead of the town, all the dead towns of the cemetery that was Europe. Here they are, at the timeless twilight hour, pilgrims all, invading the Temple of which they are both fiery foundation and guardians. . . . For they have no tombs to hold them back, no cemeteries to bind them to the earth." *A Beggar in Jerusalem.* New York: Random House, 1970, p. 201.

82. Pisar, *Of Blood and Hope,* p. 288.

83. Pisar, *La Ressource humaine,* pp. 249, 242.

84. Pisar, *Of Blood and Hope,* pp. 205–209.

85. Pisar, *La Ressource humaine,* p. 201.

86. Cargas, p. 62.

87. *Ibid.*, p. 86.

88. Lejeune, *Le Pacte autobiographique,* p. 173.

Art of the Holocaust: A Summary

Sybil Milton

Until recently, art produced during the Holocaust has been viewed as a historical and aesthetic curiosity, rather than as a central element in understanding the history of those persecuted by the Nazis. Even today, we are still disconcerted that conditions that barely supported life could result in the creation of works of high aesthetic quality and beauty. The relationship between a flourishing clandestine culture (art, mustic, theater, and literature) and the brutality of the milieu in which it was produced, has led to two general misconceptions: (1) a pragmatic fear that art could be used as an alibi minimizing the horrors; and (2) a simplistic and vague identification of works of art with so-called "spiritual resistance." The relationship between art and atrocity, although not yet fully understood, influences our perception of World War II just as at the time it enabled the artists to retain their individuality under conditions of extreme duress. Thus, M. Koscielniak, a Polish inmate artist in Auschwitz, stated: "The desire and aim of the SS was to create a prisoner who submitted to the continuing terror of the camp without thought, without initiative, following every order. We quickly escaped this through jokes, songs, poems, irony, and caricature."[1]

Art of the Holocaust does *not* refer to a single school, generation, or national style of art. It includes art produced by professionals in certain settings between 1933 and 1945: in concentration camps, ghettos, transit and labor camps, prisons, resistance, and in hiding places throughout Nazi occupied Europe from the Pyrenées to the Urals. The artist and victim were one and the same person; unlike Goya, Daumier, Grosz, or Picasso, the artists trapped in the Holocaust were not simply witnesses or social critics. Artists could not work openly, nor could they exhibit in galleries or museums. The victim-artists were their own chroniclers, historians, dealers, archivists, and consumers. They had to improvise materials for clandestine work by

filching canvas and color from labor assignments that provided access
to paper in SS offices, kitchens, or on the black market that existed
in every camp and ghetto. Charcoal, rust, watered ink, food, and
vegetable dyes often provided color and line. Drawings were made
on the backs of SS circulars, reports and medical forms; on wrapping
paper and tissue paper, and even on the perforated blank margins
of postage stamps.[2] Drawings were also completed on recycled paper
pockmarked with SS bullet holes from target practice.[3]

Art survived not only because of conscious planning but also by
fortunate accident. A corpus of approximately 30,000 drawings, sketches,
oils, watercolors, and sculptures (about 14 percent of the total number
of works created) still existed in 1945. While most artists are judged
by a selection carefully culled from the finished products of their
creative labors, the artists of the Holocaust are frequently judged on
preliminary sketches and studies for works that were never completed.
Sometimes the works were unsigned and the artist unknown.

Surviving art can be divided into five broad categories. The largest
single group (nearly 25 percent of the total) were portraits. This is
not surprising, since diaries and documents attest to the fact that this
was the most common genre. Portraits had a magical meaning in this
setting (as also in many native and folk art forms). They gave the
subject a sense of permanent presence among the living, extremely
important when temporal physical presence was so fragile and tenuous.
Occasionally, portraits would also be commissioned by the Nazis as
gifts to superiors or their own families, and also for the documentation
of medical experiments. For example, Mengele commissioned a Czech
Jewish artist, Dinah Gottlievoba, to do portraits of gypsy prisoners
as illustrations for a book he had hoped to publish about his medical
experiments in Auschwitz.[4] Leo Haas, Halina Olomucki, and Arnold
Daghani also reported having received orders to do portraits of their
Nazi tormentors, often from photographs of Nazi relatives missing
in action. If the resulting work was acceptable, it often helped secure
more lenient work assignments or better rations.[5]

After the German Communist artist Karl Schwesig was arrested
in July 1933, he was initially beaten and dumped in the basement
of the Düsseldorf restaurant *Schlegelkeller*, literally translated as "cellar
of blows." After being remanded into police custody, he was sentenced
to 16 months in jail. In his subsequent autobiographical cycle about
his experiences, published in 1935–36, Schwesig noted that "all my
fellow inmates received portraits as presents for their wives, who
took the sketches, when they brought clean linen and food on visiting
days."[6]

Artists also conveyed their own plight through self-portraiture. During his internment in St. Cyprien, and throughout his subsequent three and one-half years in hiding in Brussels, the German Jewish artist Felix Nussbaum completed numerous self-portraits that conveyed his terror and isolation. Two works from 1943 are especially relevant for showing the role of portraiture in resisting depersonalization. One self-portrait showed Nussbaum with yellow star and Belgian Jewish identity card containing his photograph, although in reality he never registered and never wore a yellow star. These symbols of oppression and segregation showed Nussbaum's total identification with the fate of his Jewish coreligionists. The second self-portrait showed an unclothed Nussbaum at his easel; in the foreground are four paint flasks. Three are labeled "humor, nostalgia, and suffering"; the fourth is marked poison.[7] Unlike the first self-portrait, Nussbaum wears neither a shabby coat nor a Jewish star; he presents himself in his essence: an artist. The depiction of one's own or another person's likeness, without abstraction or symbolization, was a cohesive metaphor for the value of individual life juxtaposed to the depersonalized mass terror of Nazi-occupied Europe. All art functioned as a bond and common language, and portraits, in particular, created a means of communication and a sense of community among the victims as well as a language of visual communication and a means of understanding for posterity.

The second category of Holocaust art consists of drawings of inanimate objects, including landscapes showing the bucolic countryside outside Theresienstadt or the snowcapped Pyrenées mountains behind Gurs. Landscapes tended to reinforce the artists' memories and strengthened connections to a world outside the concentration camp universe. Thus, Karl Schwesig wrote in his memoirs of the southern French transit camps: "All pain and suffering could have been forgotten in the southern French landscape of vineyards and mountains, had I brought watercolors, pencils, and paper."[8] Among the drawings containing inanimate objects are numerous still lives produced in ghettos and in hiding, showing vacant attics crammed with abandoned property and windows overlooking courtyards and streets where raids and deportations were taking place. There were also architectural sketches showing the similar physical layout of virtually every camp, always surrounded by barbed wire, watch towers, and closed gates. These works formed nearly 20 percent of the surviving art.[9]

The third type of art was evidentiary art. Thus Karl Schwesig's miniatures show the daily life of internees in Gurs and Noé and sketches by the Austrian artist Kurt Conrad Loew showed the me-

ticulous weighing of portions of bread in St. Cyprien. Furthermore,
Felix Nussbaum drew the ramshackle hut that served as the synagogue
in St. Cyprien during 1940. Other drawings portrayed conditions and
scenes in camps about whose history we know very little, as for
example, Compiègne in occupied northern France, Fossoli in northern
Italy, and Falkensee, a satellite camp of Sachsenhausen in Germany.
Evidentiary art ranged from generic pictures depicting camp life (roll
calls, selections, tortures, food distribution, and forced labor) to specific,
albeit universalized, images of extreme deprivation, such as the single
skeletal corpse tattoed with his inmate registration number by Leon
Delarbre in Buchenwald or Zoran Music in Dachau. This number
served as a means of identification. This type of thematic art is found
in about 20 percent of the surviving works.

The fourth and fifth types of surviving art, caricatures (20 percent)
and abstracts (15 percent), show the artists' ability to distance themselves from their surroundings and even to mock it with vitriolic
humor. Most of these works were relatively small in size (usually 6
× 9 inches or less) and drawn in pencil, ink, or primary colors.
Bertalan Göndör drew pencil cartoons on the blank sides of censored
postcards mailed to his wife from the labor camps in eastern Hungary
and the Czech artist Cisar filled a small notebook with blue-ink
satirical sketches of daily life in Dachau. Hans Reichel produced 42
abstracts in watercolors in his notebook (later published under the
title *Cahier de Gurs*) during the summer of 1942.[10] The diary accompanying these drawings correlates conditions to color selections and
the abstractions of flora and fauna found near the transit camp.

Other art works included stage sets for cabaret and theater per-
formances in Theresienstadt and illustrations for song books produced
in Buchenwald and the Moor camps. Sculpture produced in Buchenwald, Hinzert, and Maidanek also survived. Moreover, many artists,
like Adolf Frankl in Vienna, began to paint only after the war ended;
others repainted their lost drawings from memory. A few artists like
Leo Haas, Herbert Sandberg, and Zoran Music returned to camp
themes in their postwar painting cycles; for example, the series *Nous
ne sommes pas les derniers* by Zoran Music combined themes of atomic
annihilation with subjects from Dachau reflecting the incorporation
of his memories of extreme suffering with contemporary concerns.

Illegal art as well as officially commissioned art even came to the
attention of the Auschwitz camp commandant Rudolf Hoess, who
complained that "prisoners are to be used for useful labor, since art
leads to an irresponsible and wasteful use of materials that are difficult
to get. I also prohibit all black market work, all senseless pieces of

kitsch, irrespective of the rank of the SS personnel who order such work." [Order No. 24 of 8 July 1942]. Obviously compulsory work produced by inmate artists was meticulously executed and technically excellent, since the interned artists' fate depended on compliance with SS orders and whims. It is probable that assigned art did not result in any significant aesthetic works, although the portraits of the perpetrators were occasionally used for purposes of identification in postwar criminal prosecutions.

The surviving art shows no geographical distinctions in themes between eastern ghettos and concentration camps and western transit camps. However, it does show several iconographic distinctions based on gender. Women artists seem to have painted a substantially larger number of children's portraits and collective scenes in camp infirmaries, showing small groups of women helping each other. These thematic distinctions are not accidental. Recent research about women and the Holocaust indicates that art reflected reality; thus, mothers and small children were usually treated together during the deportations and selections, and women were usually assigned to care for those children who survived in the camps. Moreover, patterns of survival reveal that women provided mutual help and support in small groups of nonbiological families, increasing their chances of survival.[11] Women also painted fewer satiric and abstract drawings, reflecting their subordinate position and late appearance in most twentieth century avant-garde art movements.

Clandestine art that survived reflected the conditions of daily terror across continental Europe between 1939 and 1945. It is presumptuous to assume that any work of art could change the course of history or prevent future genocides, yet the enduring humanism of Holocaust art restores our sense of balance in confronting the official war art and stereotypes that prevailed in Nazi propaganda. It also fills the gap in twentieth century art history for the decades of the 1930s and 1940s. The surviving documentation is not anonymous and offers us the possibility of a direct understanding of the conditions and setting in which individual artists worked. Holocaust art as a pedagogical tool enables us to study all aspects of Holocaust history: the persecution of Jews, clandestine resistance, the mixture of nationalities and prisoner types in every European concentration camp, and the nature of life in hiding. With the passage of time and the creation of postwar artistic traditions, the art of the Holocaust has joined art about the Holocaust in forming a new socially critical contemporary artistic tradition.

NOTES

1. M. Koscielniak, *Bilder von Auschwitz*. Frankfurt, Nov. 1982, unpaginated exhibit catalog.

2. Herbert Remmert *and* Peter Barth, *Karl Schwesig: Leben und Werk*. Berlin and Dusseldorf, 1984, pp. 91–92 and 96.

3. See the works of Boris Taslitzky, discussed in Janet Blatter *and* Sybil Milton, *Art of the Holocaust*. New York, 1981, p. 266.

4. Blatter *and* Milton, *Art of the Holocaust*, p. 249.

5. Mary Costanza, *The Living Witness: Art in the Concentration Camps and Ghettos*. New York and London, 1982, pp. 21–51.

6. See Karl Schwesig, *Schlegelkeller*. Berlin and Dusseldorf: Remmert and Barth Gallery, 1983.

7. Peter Junk *and* Wendelin Zimmer, Felix Nussbaum: Leben und Werk. Cologne and Bramsche, 1982, p. 253. (Illus. # 277 and 278.)

8. Remmert *and* Barth, *Karl Schwesig*, p. 89.

9. Blatter *and* Milton, Art of the Holocaust, passim.

10. Hans Reichel, *Cahier de Gurs*. Geneva, 1974.

11. Sybil Milton, "Women and the Holocaust: The Case of German and German-Jewish Women" *When Biology Became Destiny: Women in Weimar and Nazi Germany*. Renate Bridenthal, Atina Grossmann, *and* Marion Kaplan, *eds*. New York, 1984, pp. 297–333.

Jewish Art and Artists in the Shadow of the Holocaust

Luba Krugman Gurdus

Among the thousands of art works which surfaced in Europe after the end of World War II, the Jewish share, of immense documentary value and consequence, was of surprisingly small volume. It was almost inconceivable that the six years of collective clandestine recording resulted in such insignificant output. The major reason for this phenomenon was, however, in conformity with the determination of the Nazis to obliterate all possible traces of their crimes against the Jews. Thus art, reflecting the gruesome reality of systematic victimization, seen through the eyes of most sensitive witnesses, became a major target of the ruthless perpetrator.

Jewish artists were exposed to persecution and violence and their art works were destroyed. Even those who temporarily served the Nazis were murdered or deported to death camps after they outlived their usefulness. Artists who survived the Holocaust had a minimal chance to retrieve their clandestine work, lost, burned, or buried under rubble. The only sizable body of clandestine art was recovered in the model ghetto of Teresin, Czechoslovakia, while smaller caches were found in the transit camps of Western Europe.

In Poland, the intense Nazi terror, provoked a compelling urge for immediate response. But the stringent orders, causing the problems of dislocation and survival, killed the will and impeded the initiative. After settling in sealed ghettos, many artists became seriously involved in the rescue process and education of the young and in an effort to sustain the rapidly ebbing morale of the ghetto population.

The surviving oeuvre, far from a comprehensive visual record of the ghetto or camp experience, reflects, nevertheless, the Jewish ordeal in poignant examples of spontaneous reaction and emotional response to the unprecedented spiritual torment of victims, exposed to indifference, isolation, and impending doom. This precious artistic legacy, deeply rooted in the Jewish drama, includes straightforward recordings of honest testimony, conceived in simple, unadorned styles and techniques. Their visual aspect and emotional impact are painfully memorable. They expose the awful truth of the Holocaust with immediacy and sensitivity in portraits marked by suffering, deeply ingrained in the faces of the tormented and in images of mass transfers and deportations, pulsating with agony and despair. The value of these art works supersedes aesthetic judgment and is primarily documentary. They should, therefore, be viewed not only against the stylistic trends they reflect but also against the indelible events they relate and the moral dilemmas they raise.

When the Germans invaded Poland, artists' unions were disbanded as most members were drafted into the army. Upon demobilization, the ill-organized union of Jewish artists, headed in Warsaw by Feliks Frydman, shrunk and was in a state of disarray because of Nazi manhunts and registration requirements for Jews, who were subsequently dispatched to labor camps.

The imminent danger sent many Jewish artists to the Soviet-occupied zone of Eastern Poland. Those who stayed in the German-occupied area turned for assistance to their Polish colleagues but learned that they were not welcome in the emerging underground movement, subsidized from abroad. Their hope for a joint response to a mutual enemy soon waned. The pre-war discrimination against Jews, intensified by the surge of anti-Jewish doctrines, undermined the bonds and friendships between Jews and Poles. Consequently, the resettlement into tightly sealed ghettos automatically severed all ties with the Polish artistic community.

Between October 2 and November 15, 1940, half a million Jews of Warsaw were confined to a restricted area which was carved off several times while its population increased by the flow of refugees from neighboring hamlets and deportees from Germany, Austria, and Czechoslovakia. During its initial stage, the Warsaw Ghetto developed an active cultural life. Its theaters opened doors to an eager public and its artists found employment as stage and costume designers. Several printing presses issued newspapers with added bulletins for satirical comments and caricatures. This illegal literature, freely circulated behind the ghetto walls, caught the attention of the Nazis who clamped down on the clandestine activities by closing all printing shops and wiping out the artists and printers in random executions.[1]

After sealing off the ghettos, the Nazis declared illegal the professions of all artists and intellectuals who ultimately became a burden to social welfare. In Warsaw, The Jewish Society for Social Welfare (ZTOS) was headed by the eminent historian Emanuel Ringelblum.

The society—in charge of health care, hygiene, entertainment, and education—soon evolved a cultural society (JYKOR), supervised by Rachel Auerbach, Abraham Guterman, Sonia Nowogrodzki, and Shakne Zagan.[2] The Cultural Society established an Entertainment Committee which extended financial support to artists of every vocation and skill. In November of 1940, it also opened a School of Applied Graphics and Technology at Sienna 16, with Otto Axner, David Greiffenberg, and J. Berkner heading the faculty. The school offered a variety of courses including architectural design and history of art. Soon, however, the efforts of the faculty were seriously curtailed by the Nazis, under the assumption that the pursuit of culture was in itself an act of defiance. After the school was shut, its activities were partly restored at Grzybowska, where it was attended by eighty students of various age. It remained under the direction of Greiffenberg who inspired the production of a students' mural on a wall surrounding a kindergarten.

When this school was again liquidated by the Nazis, art teachers responded with courage and determination and began using the facilities of the Economic Club for Artists, at Orla 6, for lectures, concerts and art courses for the young. The initiatives of the club proved beneficial and Roman Rozenthal, who contributed to its usefulness, was honored by a retrospective exhibition, marking twenty years of his artistic activity and his exemplary service at the Union of Jewish Artists in Poland.[3]

During the deportations of August 1942, the club's membership shrunk and the remaining artists joined the Practical Worshop, temporarily authorized by the Nazis. Maintained by the Union of Jewish Craftsmen, the workshop produced a variety of carved items for practical use. It was directed by Wladyslaw Weintraub, assisted by Hersz Cyna and Henryk Rabinowicz. During the continuing deportations the workshop was raided and its members taken to Treblinka.[4]

Very few ghetto artists had a chance to exercise their professional skills. The majority worked in education or sought employment on communal projects. One was the decoration of the Community Center, supervised by the painter and graphic artist Maximilian Eljowicz, assisted by Szymon Trachter, Abraham Ostrzega, and Jozef Sliwniak. The extensive project, never completed, was strongly endorsed by Adam Czerniakow, the chief of the *Judenrat*, who belonged to a small group of art patrons, sympathetic to the artists' plight and eager to enlist their service for a record on the Nazi reign of terror.[5]

The Warsaw Ghetto housed a great number of gifted artists. Outstanding among them was Roman Kramsztyk, associated with the School of Paris. Visiting his ailing mother in Warsaw, he was forced

by the Nazis into the ghetto, where he created a remarkable series
of drawings which caused controversy on both sides of the wall.[6]
Smuggled out to the Aryan part of the city, the shattering images
touched off a spontaneous response from the Polish artistic community.[7]
Kramsztyk's "Old Jew with Children", 1942, Warsaw (ZIH, Warsaw),
became a symbol of the children's plight. It portrays a robust vagabond,
carrying a little girl and flanked by two destitute boys clinging to
him. The image reflects a sense of imminent drama in a singular
merger of feeling and expression conveying the artist's insight into
one of the most disturbing ghetto problems.

The lot of the homeless ghetto children, whose numbers grew daily,
served as a persistent reminder of the appalling conditions. Their
numbers were so staggering that the police were forced to open a
special institution for them, though CENTOS (Central Organization
for the Protection of Children and Orphans) and YYGA (Jewish Social
Self-aid Society) couldn't do more to alleviate the rapidly spreading
misery.[8]

Maurycy Bromberg, another ghetto artist, captured the lot of the
Jewish child, in close relation to the acute problems of repeated
transfers and dislocations. In his "Watching the Transport," undated,
Warsaw (ZIH, Warsaw), the artist isolated a child from a throng of
people, jamming a ghetto gate, in painful allusion to its loneliness
and to traditional Jewish isolation. The work harks back to the dramatic
compositions of Joseph Israels and Leonid Pasternak, created in Russia
after the 1905 Kishinev pogrom. These visual comments on the
mounting hostility toward Jews, branded as "enemies of the people,"
who can be murdered with impunity, served the Nazis as incentive
for the total extermination of the Jews.

Genia (Gela) Seksztajn-Lichtensztajn, a ghetto artist and educator,
was in the forefront of an effort to draw the attention of the ghetto
dwellers to the desperate situation of the children. Her sensitive
portraits of emaciated homeless and dying ghetto beggars, aimlessly
roaming the streets, reflected the catastrophic situation and her own
despair. Aware of the children's fate and her own predicament, she
wrote on August 1, 1942 in her will:

> "Now I am at peace, I must perish but I have done what I could, I
> have attempted to hide a testament of my works.
>   Be well my colleagues and friends, be well Jewish people and never
> again allow such tragedies to occur.[9]

Gela's husband, Israel, who hid her works with the Ringelblum
Archives, wrote in his testament, dated July 31, 1942:

I want my wife to be remembered, Gela Seksztajn, artist, dozens of works. . . . During the three years of war, worked with children as educator, teacher, made stage sets, costumes for the children's productions, received awards. Now, together with me, we are preparing to receive death.[10]

Gela's diary and her art works, including the "Beggar Girl" and "Girl in Rags" both, ca. 1942, Warsaw (ZIH, Warsaw), survived the Holocaust and reveal her effort to leave a trace of the children's suffering and pain, sealed in the girls' eyes, and her own resillience in fighting the steady upsurge of Nazi terror. Finally, her husband's testament attests to her self-sacrifice in her task of educator and implores for remembrance, the last aspiration of the doomed Jews.

The profusion of portraits in the artists' legacy is an explicit connotation to a universal urge for remembrance. Lea Lilienblum, who survived the Warsaw Ghetto, produced a memorable "Portrait of Yitzhak Kazenelson," 1943, Warsaw (GFH, Israel), seemingly inspired by the poet's personality. In a truly Expressionist fervor, she captured the striking likeness of the prophetic bard, whose "Song of the Murdered Jewish People" became a lasting monument to Jewish martyrdom.

Larger Jewish ghettos in Poland, housed colonies of artists, most of whom perished and very scarce data remain about them. The Ghetto of Lodz had its House of Culture, opened in March 1941 for 60 musicians and painters. Among them were two excellent portraitists, Hirsh Szylis and Itzhak Brauer, both employed by the chief of the Jewish Council, Chaim Rumkowski. Szylis survived the war and became famous for his haunting ghetto scenes, which he still paints. In Lodz he represented Rumkowski as protector of the ghetto children.[11]

The Lodz Ghetto also had an Artists' Union, known as "Start," which included among its members, Henoch Barczynski, Maks Haneman, Pola Lindenfeld, Maurycy Trombacz, Szymon Sherman, and Amos Szwarc.[12] Not unlike Kramsztyk, Bromberg, and Seksztajn, Amos Szwarc expressed concern for the destitute ghetto orphans in his "Children in the Lodz Ghetto," 1944, Lodz (GFH, Israel). The artist was deported to Auschwitz where he perished. Szymon Szerman, who died in the ghetto, created a truly monumental "Transfer to the Ghetto," 1940, Lodz (GFH, Israel). The perfectly balanced pattern, conceived in earthy, dark hues, renders the gloomy atmosphere of the massive event. Josef Kowner, who was murdered in Auschwitz, left a haunting episode of a transfer in his "Carrying Feces," undated, Lodz (ZIH, Warsaw). The artist singled out a group of Jews, pushing their meager belongings to their new destination. The sparingly illuminated scene and the artist's expert handling of textures add to the traumatic effect of the nostalgic picture. Finally, Sara Gliksman-Fajtlowicz, who survived the war, created an impressionist image of a "Deportation to Lodz," 1940, Lodz (Yad Vashem, Israel), conveying the monumental chaos and confusion associated with the event.

Hirsh Szylis, mentioned above, portrayed a "Deportation to Lodz," undated, Lodz (Yad Vashem, Israel). The artist put the main emphasis on the damage caused by the cruelty and brutality of the perpetrators, who left behind scattered Jewish possessions, an empty children's carriage, broken chairs, a ladder leading to the attic of the abandoned house. His interest in intense light, subdued color, and expert handling of detail add to the poignancy of the scene.

The Jewish artists who in 1939 escaped to the Eastern, Soviet-occupied zone of Poland reached Bialystok, Vilna, and Lvov. Some reached Kovno in Lithuania, where an official Art Workshop remained under the auspices of the Jewish Council and was headed by its deputy secretary, Abraham Golub-Tory. The latter, responsible for the hiding of the ghetto archives, was instrumental in preserving the art of Esther Lurie and Benzion Josef Szmidt, known as "Nolick." During the liquidation of the Kovno Ghetto, Nolick perished in a bunker, but his remarkable drawings of deportation and ghetto life were recovered, as were those of Jacob Lifschitz, who was murdered in Dachau, and Sali Becker, who died in 1941. Esther Lurie, survived the war but retrieved only a fraction of her large Holocaust output, recording life in the Kovno Ghetto. Vilna, an important pre-war center of Jewish culture, conducted an active ghetto life. Through the initiative of Jacob Gens, the chief of the Jewish Council, a Culture House was established at 6 Strashun Street. The Council also subsidized a Union of Writers and Artists, which became a center of intellectual and artistic activity.[13]

Persistent Nazi pressures encouraged the vigorous output of clandestine art under the guidance of Jacob Szer, an established artist and educator. Nahum Rombeck, H. Bahelfer, David Lankowski, and F. Segal collaborated with Szer. All perished, although Szer was temporarily spared, until he too outlived his usefulness as a portraitist and was deported by the Nazis for annihilation. An early victim was Nathan Korzen, who was hanged while his studio was set on fire.[14] Two younger artists, Samuel Bak and Alexander Bogen, survived and now live in Israel.

An intensive clandestine activity was developed in Bialystok by the local Artists' Union, joined by the enormous influx of refugees from the German-occupied zone of Poland. They included known artists like Abraham Berman, Stefania Centwerszner, Izaak Krzeczanowski, Natalia Landau, and Jakub Tynowicki. However, in anticipation of the Nazi advance into the Soviet zone in June 1941, the Artists' Union was disbanded and some artists were evacuated to Russia. Others were herded by the Nazis into the ghetto and worked in a Copies Center, formed for the reproduction of masterpieces stolen by the Nazis from major European museums and private collections. Izak Celniker, a member of the workshop, mentions that at least ten artists were used for producing forgeries of works by Rubens, Murillo, and Boecklin for resale in other countries. During the liquidation of the ghetto, most artists joined the armed resistance and perished or were deported to Treblinka. Only a few succeeded in escaping to the woods and joining partisans.

Y. Charyton survived the massacre and created a series of sketches demonstrating the Nazi reign of terror. His scene of deportation, "Jews Pushed to the Transport," 1942, Bialystok (ZIH, Warsaw), pulsates with fear and frenzy. The annotation, appearing on the sketch, names the place of the event and comments on the brutality of the mounted Nazi.

Chaim Urison, who was killed in Bialystok in August 1943, during a deportation to Treblinka, was also active in the Copies Center. A known portraitist, he created the "Ghetto Jew," 1942, Bialystok (GFH, Israel), a pathetic study full of human content. The Jew's eyes, staring of deep sockets with deep emotion, reflect the hopeless situation of the ghetto.

The exodus from the Generalgouvernement brought to Lvov a great number of artists who congregated around the cooperative "Hudoznik" (Artist), headed by Jonas Stern. The group included Martin Katz and Karol Ferster, editors of the satirical periodical *Krokodyl* (Crocodile) and Gela Rozmus and Marjan Wnuk, teaching at the Lvov Academy of Fine Arts. In June 1941, some artists were evacuated to Russia. Those who stayed, were mercilessly murdered by the Nazis who burned Otto Hahn alive. Many perished in random executions; others committed suicide.[15] During the liquidation of the ghetto, Jonas Stern was deported to Janowo. His "Street in the Lwow Ghetto," 1944, Lvov (ZIH, Warsaw), re-creates the hopeless and repressive ghetto atmosphere.

In the ghettos of Poland and Lithuania, Jewish artists were not deterred or discouraged by Nazi violence, torture, or death. Their persistent effort yielded a sizable oeuvre which was, however, destroyed by the Nazis' frenzy to annihilate every record of their crime against humanity. Most art works disappeared, either consumed by fire or buried under rubble. Nevertheless, the miraculously salvaged examples convey the ghetto drama and the brutal methods of dehumanization and victimization. They stand out through their distinct subject matter and are imbued with deep emotion, which even the most stringent self-restraint could not stifle. The combined oeuvre is, however, so exceedingly small that it does not approach the volume of works produced in a single ghetto, deliberately set up by the Nazis in a Moravian fortress, which became known as the Ghetto of Teresin.

The Ghetto of Theresienstadt (Teresin), soon became known as "Die Stadt, die Hitler den Juden schenkte" (The city presented by Hitler to the Jews). This "model ghetto" was created to deceive public opinion and to camouflage Hitler's real intentions. Set up for "deserving Jews," the ghetto was open to outside inspection and thus permitted an extensive cultural life with theater, orchestra, and art workshop. The Nazis used ghetto artists for special assignments and thus unwittingly also supplied them with materials for clandestine work. Disregarding risk, most artists engaged in secret activity and some were caught in the known "Affair of Four." It involved Felix Bloch, who died after torture in the Small Fortress; Otto Ungar, who was sent to Buchenwald; and Bedrich Fritta and Leo Haas, both dispatched to Auschwitz. Only Haas survived and returned to Teresin to retrieve his 400 drawings, hidden in the walls of the ghetto. In his enormous work, Haas represented all facets of the hopeless ghetto life. His "General Distribution of Food, Post BV," 1944, Teresin (GFH, Israel), is a masterpiece of conception and execution. Similarly prolific were Otto Ungar, an art teacher from Brno, Bedrich Fritta, a commercial artist from Prague, as well as Fritz Nagel, whose 200 drawings were found in an attic. Very productive were also Malvina Schalkova, Dinah Gottliebova and Charlotte Buresova. The latter stated in a postwar interview: "What was most terrible, more terrible than hunger and indecent lodging, was the unknown tomorrow, the trains to the East."[16] Due to relatively bearable conditions, the Teresin output was enormous and a substantial part of it reached posterity.

Comparable efforts, on a reduced scale, may be discerned in transit camps with Jewish inmates. Scattered throughout Western Europe, these camps fulfilled the function of Theresienstadt, keeping prisoners in closely guarded centers from which they were eventually dispatched to annihilation camps. Many gifted artists, confined to these camps, were motivated by an urge to assert their existence and left traces of their identity. In Drancy, France, Aizik Feder completed a remarkable series of signed and annotated portraits of his fellow inmates, and also himself. In Gurs, France, Felix Nussbaum re-created the camp conditions in allegorical compositions, completed outside the camp. Leon Landau, Jacques Ochs, and Irene Awret worked in Malines, Belgium. Arnold Daghani created a series of important works in

Transnistria, Romania, Bertalan Gondor worked in Volocz, Hungary and Walter Pinto in Westerbork, Holland. Most of them were dispatched to extermination camps where they perished.[17]

There is no trace of any activity in the extermination camps of Poland. Jews brought to Chelmno or Belzec were soon murdered and very few escaped from Treblinka, Sobibor, and Majdanek. Jewish artists succeeded in producing some clandestine work in labor camps outside Poland but their combined output was minimal and disappeared among the numerous art works which surfaced in these camps after the war. The reason for this discrepancy is not analyzed or discussed. It is an established fact that not all prisoners were treated alike. Jews were exposed to rigorous selections and the most fit were only temporarily exempt from gassing. Subsequently, assigned to hard labor, they were kept in separate barracks and denied all privileges. In the same camps, inmates of other nationalities were treated with more leniency.

In Auschwitz, only single Jews were used by the Nazis for special assignments and were able to divert some of their art supplies for clandestine work. One of them was Leo Haas, who was assigned to producing counterfeit money; another, Dinah Gottliebova, was ordered by Dr. Mengele to portray the gypsies in the camp. Jewish artists, deprived of these exceptional opportunities, were forced to search Nazi trashcans for any type of material which would take an image, while Poles, inmates in Auschwitz, were allowed to build a camp museum and subsequently had free access to art supplies. Despite these conditions Maurycy Bromberg, deported from the Warsaw Ghetto to Auschwitz, succeeded in creating one of the most chilling images of Jewish martyrdom. His "Five Jews in one Yoke," undated, Auschwitz (ZIH, Warsaw), is a most poignant indictment of Nazi cruelty and brutality.

In Buchenwald, Walter Spitzer created a monumental sketch portraying Jewish victimization. His "Distribution of Soup," 1945, Buchenwald (GFH, Israel), is a most accurate and detailed representation of the daily ritual in the camp. However, the date and the medium clearly suggest that this pen and ink drawing was in all probability produced after liberation. The same classification may be attached to the series of works by David Olère, equally dated "1945."

Quite unusual is the case of Boris Taslitzky, the only Jewish artist responsible for over 100 works, completed in Buchenwald.[18] Caught with his false identification papers, he was considered Aryan and kept together with his French colleagues, Pierre Mania and Auguste Favier.[19] Taking advantage of his special situation, he recorded the Jewish ordeal in the camp. In his "Little Camp, Feb. 1945," 1945,

Buchenwald (The Artist's Coll.), Taslitzky shows the mass massacre and open graves in Buchenwald. His friend Mania expressed his outrage at the Jewish suffering in his "Infirmary Barracks," 1943, Buchenwald (The Artist's Coll.) and so did Favier in his "Block in the Little Camp," 1943, Buchenwald (Robert Favier Coll.). The interest of these two Frenchmen in the Jewish ordeal was also shared by several Poles, among them Karol Konieczny and Jozef Szajna in Buchenwald and Waldemar Nowakowski in Auschwitz. The latter created "The Jews' Last Road," 1943, Auschwitz (Janina Jaworska Coll., Warsaw), where he shows a row of emaciated Jews, lined up for the crematorium. These examples of great documentary value supplement the minimal Jewish camp output in a most poignant manner.

The collective oeuvre from transit camps and long-range extermination camps adds considerably to the record of the Jewish ordeal with hasty sketches of selections, food lines, and torture before extermination. These tragic images alternate with sensitive portraits and self-portraits, used to perpetuate likeness. They reveal the artists' increasing awareness of impending doom and their emotional response to the imminent catastrophe. While the ghetto scenes were imbued with despair, those from the camps are permeated with agony. In close parallel, the ghetto drawings show great care for documentary evidence while the camp sketches are summary, betraying haste and tension.

Bound by common subject matter, they are also marked by a conventional academic realism rarely affected by the stylistic trends, prevailing in contemporary European art. Nevertheless, the portraits of Gela Seksztajn and Lea Lilienblum betray a marked affinity with the Expressionist representations of Chaim Soutine and Oscar Kokoschka and the art of Otto Ungar is deeply rooted in the Expressionism of Otto Dix and George Grosz. Most works are purely objective but the emotion underlying each effort adds to a cumulative intensity generating from the collective oeuvre which offers a unique perspective on the Holocaust, viewed through the eyes of artists who found strength to record their own tragedy. The great majority of Jewish artists perished; they seem to have realized all along that their work had greater meaning than life itself. Pain and suffering emanate from the miraculously salvaged pages. Retrieved by survivors, they reached posterity with their meaningful message. They touched the conscience of humanity and instilled reverent homage for the creators who succeeded in capturing the very last vestiges of the Jewish world, rapidly dissipating in the shadows of the Holocaust.

NOTES

1. Alexander Donat, *The Holocaust Kingdom*. (New York: Holocaust Library, 1976), p. 44.

2. Janina Jaworska, *Polska Sztuka Walczaca* (Polish Fighting Art) Warsaw: Wydawnictwa Artystyczne i Filmowe, 1976, p. 104.

3. Jonas Turkow, *Azoy is es gewesen* (Thus It Happened). 1948, p. 202.

4. Jaworska (see note 2), p. 106. The following artists perished in the August 1942 deportation: Leokadja Bereger, Abraham Frydman, Chaim Funtonowicz, David Greiffenberg, Adam Herszaft, Henryk Rabinowicz, Erna Rotman and Nathan Spiegel.

5. *Ibid.*, p. 106. During the liquidation of the Warsaw Ghetto, several Jewish artists escaped to the Aryan part of the city. Some of them had been recognized and turned over to the Gestapo, among others, Julia Rinegel-Keil, Lidia Szole-Karakasz and Jakub Bickels.

6. *Ibid.*, p. 107. The art works of Roman Kramsztyk, smuggled out from the Ghetto, were sold by his friends, Wanda Polkowska and Leonard Pekalski.

7. *Ibid.*, p. 108. Felicjan Kowarski created several drawings, depicting the deplorable condition in the ghetto: "Hunger in the Ghetto" and "Israelite," 1943, Warsaw (National Museum, Warsaw).

8. Yiddish Scientific Institute, New York. *Underground Cultural Work in the Jewish Ghettos of Poland. A Report from Warsaw, dated May 20, 1944.*

9. Yosef Sandel, "Umgekomene Yidishe Kunstler" (Jewish Artists Who Perished). *Yiddish Buch* (Jewish Book). Warsaw, 1957, vol. 1, pp. 237–238. Translated from Yiddish by Yitzchak Mais.

10. Ruta Sakowska, ed., *Archiwum Ringelbluma. Getto Warszawskie, lipiec 1942-styczen 1943* (Warsaw Ghetto, August 1942-January 1943) (National Scientific Institute, 1980), p. 106, document 49, dated August 31, 1942, Israel Lichtensztajn's Notes and Testament. Translated from the Polish by the writer.

11. Isaiah Trunk, *Judenrat*. New York: Macmillan, 1972, p. 371, illustration.

12. *Ibid.*, pp. 225–227.

13. Vilna Album Committee, *Jerusalem of Lithuania*. Egg Harbor City, NJ: Laurete Press, 1974, pp. 460–468, illustration.

14. Tel-Aviv Museum, *Jewish Artists Who Perished. Memorial Exhibition.* Tel-Aviv: Tel-Aviv Museum, April-May, 1968.

15. Jaworska (see note 2), p. 132. Killed in random executions were Emil Schinagel, Erno Erb, Jozef Kaganus, Martin Katz, Mendel Reif, and Julia Archer; Zygmunt Balk and Grzegorz Polak committed suicide.

16. Dawidowicz, Freudenheim, Nowitch, *Spiritual Resistance*: Art from Concentration Camps: 1940–1945. New York: Union of American Hebrew Congregations, 1981, p. 54.

17. Aizik Feder perished in 1943 in Auschwitz; Felix Nussbaum perished in 1944 in Auschwitz; Leon Landau perished in 1944 in Bergen-Belsen; Bertalan Gondor perished in 1944 in Mauthausen; Walter Pinto perished under unknown circumstances.

18. Boris Taslitzky, *111 Dessins Faits*. Paris: Edition Hautefeuille, 1978.

19. A. Favier and P. Mania, *Buchenwald: Scenes Prises sur le vif de Horreurs Nazis.* Lyons: Federation Nationale de Deportes et Interns, Resistants et Patriotes, 1946.

ABBREVIATIONS

ZIH (Zydowski Instytut Historyczny): Jewish Historical Institute (Warsaw).
GFH: Ghetto Fighters' House (Israel).

Contributors

ALAN L. BERGER is Chairman of the Jewish Studies Program at Syracuse University. He is the author or editor of several books, including *Crisis and Covenant: The Holocaust in American Jewish Fiction* and *Methodology in the Academic Teaching of the Holocaust.* He has published numerous articles on the literature, pedagogy, and theology of post-Holocaust Judaism.

ELLEN S. FINE is Professor of French at Kingsborough Community College of The City University of New York. She is the author of *Legacy of Night: The Literary Universe of Elie Wiesel.* Her studies appeared in several books and journals, including *Writing and the Holocaust,* edited by Berel Lang, *Jewish Book Annual, Holocaust and Genocide Studies,* and *Midstream.* Professor Fine also served as a Special Adviser to the Chairman of the U.S. Holocaust Memorial Council.

EMANUEL S. GOLDSMITH is Professor of Yiddish Language and Literature at Queens College of The City University of New York. He is the author of *Modern Jewish Culture: The Story of the Yiddish Language Movement* and co-editor of *Dynamic Judaism: The Essential Writings of Mordecai M. Kaplan* and *The American Judaism of Mordecai M. Kaplan.*

LUBA K. GURDUS. An artist and art historian, Dr. Gurdus is the author of *The Death Train* and *Painful Echoes: Poems of the Holocaust. From the Diary of Luba K. Gurdus,* which contain many of her illustrations. Her articles appeared in many journals, including *Holocaust and Genocide Studies* and *Martyrdom and Resistance.* A member of the Holocaust Publications Advisory Board, Dr. Gurdus is the 1986 recipient of the First Louis E. Yavner Citizen Award from the State University of New York.

IRVING HALPERIN is Professor of English and Creative Writing at San Francisco State University. He is the author of *Messengers from the Dead: Literature of the Holocaust* and *Here I Am: A Jew in Today's*

Germany. He also contributed numerous articles, literary critiques, and short stories to such periodicals as *Christian Century, Commonweal, Judaism, Yad Vashem Studies, Studies in American Jewish Literature, Midstream,* and *New England Review.*

ROSETTE C. LAMONT is Professor of French at Queens College and a member of the doctoral faculty in the Ph.D. Program in French and the Ph.D. Program in Comparative Literature at the Graduate School and University Center of The City University of New York. She is the author of *Ionesco* and *The Two Faces of Ionesco.* Professor Lamont is a frequent contributor to the "Arts and Leisure" section of *The New York Times,* and also serves as contributing editor of *Performing Arts Journal,* and as international correspondent of *Stages.*

LAWRENCE L. LANGER is Alumnae Chair Professor of English at Simmons College in Boston. He is the author of *The Holocaust and the Literary Imagination, The Age of Atrocity: Death in Modern Literature,* and *Versions of Survival: The Holocaust and the Human Spirit.* He has a National Endowment for the Humanities Fellowship for 1989–90, to complete a book titled *The Ruins of Memory: Interpreting Holocaust Testimonies.*

SYBIL MILTON is Research Curator of the U.S. Holocaust Memorial Museum in Washington, D.C. Her publications include *Art and the Holocaust* and *Art of Jewish Children: Germany 1936–1941.* A prolific historian, Dr. Milton is also co-editor of the *Simon Wiesenthal Center Annual.*

DIANE R. SPIELMANN is the archivist of the Leo Baeck Institute in New York. She is the co-author of "Fifty Years After Kristallnacht: Another Second Generation Perspective," which appeared in *The German-Jewish Legacy in America, 1938–1988* published by the American Jewish Archives. Dr. Spielmann taught German and Judaic Studies at Queens College, Brooklyn College, and the Graduate Center of The City University of New York.

JOSEPH SUNGOLOWSKY is Professor of French Literature and Jewish Studies at Queens College, The City University of New York. He is the author of *Alfred de Vigny et le dix-huitième siècle,* and *Beaumarchais.* He has contributed articles and reviews on French Literature and Jewish Studies to various journals.

DATE DUE

'SEP 3 0 1995	
NOV 1 0 1998	
APR 1 2 2004	
OCT 1 8 2007	
OCT 2 5 2007	
NOV 2 5 2007	

DEMCO, INC. 38-2931